Extraordinary Credit Unions:

A Proven 7-Step How-to System to Unleash Breakthrough Success

Banner Press

Minneapolis, MN

copyright © Roxanne Emmerich, 2004

All rights reserved. No part of this publication may be reproduced or transmitted in any form by any means, electronic or mechanical, including photocopy, recording or any information retrieval system, without written permission from the publisher.

Printed in USA
Publisher: Banner Press
8500 Normandale Lake Blvd., Minneapolis MN 55437
Info@EmmerichGroup.com   www.EmmerichFinancial.com
Phone: 952-820-0360   FAX: 952-893-0502

USA $29.95 (Foreign $39.95)

ISBN: 1-890965-06-5

For Information about Group Purchase Pricing Call:
800.236.5885 ext. 202

Visit Our Web Site: **www.EmmerichFinancial.com**

Dedication

To my clients who invigorate me with their zest for improvement.

To Judy, Sarah, Lisa and Juanita and all my staff who rise to the occasion to do the impossible every day so that our clients can create miracles.

About the Author

Roxanne Emmerich's ability to help her financial services clients generate breakthroughs is the stuff of legend. Over 100 clients have doubled their service scores within 30 days of one visit. Over 98 percent of Sales Management and Marketing Boot Camp™ attendees asked to have an advance boot camp.

It's no surprise *Sales and Marketing Management* magazine lists her as one of the 12 most requested speakers for national sales meetings. Also, the financial services industry hails her as one of the highest rated and most in-demand speakers at their CEO and marketing conferences.

Twice voted **Entrepreneur of the Year**, Roxanne built a seven-figure company and **led one of the fastest growth, financial service startups** in the country in the 1980s.

Currently, she is president of **The Emmerich Group, Inc.**, in Minneapolis, where she works with leading edge financial institutions to advance their results.

Additional Works by the Author

Best Selling Book: *Thank God It's Monday: How to Build a Motivating Workplace*
E-Newsletter: *GrowYourBank*
Boot Camps: *Sales Management and Marketing Boot Camp*™
Summit: *Permission to Be Extraordinary*™
Video Program: *Breakthrough Sales Meetings*™

Table of Contents

Acknowledgements . . . 6

Preface: How to Read This Book . . . 8

Introduction . . . 9

Chapter 1:
 Breakthrough to Extraordinary Member Service. . . 17

Chapter 2:
 Breakthrough Vision to Outstanding Success . . . 53

Chapter 3:
 Breakthrough to Number One Positioning . . . 77

Chapter 4:
 Breakthrough Strategies to Maximize Results . . . 97

Chapter 5:
 Breakthrough to High ROI Marketing . . . 111

Chapter 6;
 Breakthrough Sales . . .163

Chapter 7:
 Breakthrough to Extraordinary High-Performance People . . . 201

Appendix . . . 249

Index . . . 290

Acknowledgements

There have been hundreds of credit union supporters who have nurtured this book. I am eternally grateful and "pay it forward" to the readers. I hope it's a blessing that stimulates a passion to be extraordinary in every person who is touched by this book.

Preface: How to Read This Book

There are many ways you can benefit from reading this book. Take the approach that best fits your needs:

Weekly Guide for Discussions and Meetings . . .

You could and should use this book to generate discussions at strategy meetings and weekly or monthly leadership meetings whereby one small element can be thought through for implementation. Ask each person on your leadership team to prepare for the meeting by reading a section and making a list of ideas they desire to implement. The book's format encourages you to make it a planning tool. Tell them to underline, highlight, and write in the book. Encourage everyone to use the book as a workbook, fill in all the blanks, and share with others.

Beginning to End . . .

You could start at the beginning and read to the end. There is a method to the madness and ordering of the chapters was given great thought. This could be a good option.

Intro to Member Service . . .

You could start with the introduction and progress to *implementing* the member service chapter. No matter what a financial institution's level of performance is, I always work on this area first. Because this is a very doable chapter and it creates a wonderful feeling of success for your people that is immediately noticeable to your clients, it is a great foundation for the other work in the book.

Choose the Area of Greatest Need . . .

Identify the area that is of most need and start with that chapter first. If you have an upcoming strategic planning meeting, make sure to read the chapters on vision, positioning, and strategy beforehand.

Introduction

This book, **Extraordinary Credit Unions**, is not for everyone. It's not for those who think they're doing an adequate job. *The extraordinary never feel like they have arrived.* It's not for those who want to make excuses about their performance. *This book is about removing the excuses.* It's not for those who are in it for the money. *Money is elusive to those who focus on it, as evidenced by Enron, World Com and many others.*

This book is for enlightened credit unions and those who want to become enlightened. It's for those who choose to be extraordinary and enjoy the thrill of being one of the best.

After working with hundreds of financial institutions over the last 15 years, I found that the differences between the extraordinary and the ordinary are consistent and extremely obvious. In fact, they are so obvious that the story compelled itself into a book.

The greatest distinction between the top performers and the rest is that the top performers are obsessed with the desire to fulfill their members' needs, dreams, and aspirations. The ordinary are focused internally on their own numbers, systems, and petty minutia.

The extraordinary constantly raise the bar and leap over tall buildings with a sense of urgency to execute their plans, while the average create a culture where excuses are accepted and "victimhood" is reinforced.

The extraordinary take time to celebrate their successes but don't let any grass grow under their feet before taking on the next level of breakthrough. The rest lay upon a carpet of complacency.

After years of working with hundreds of financial service companies, the differences became universally consistent. To verify our findings with actual data, we interviewed the very best performing organizations.

The more we researched, the more solidified were our findings. Certain elements stood out in an undeniable way that separated the extraordinary from the ordinary. The "best" have different mindsets. They are not in the transaction business. They are in the transformation business. Here is what we noticed:

- ✓ **Extraordinary Credit Unions** are passionate about their members' success. They understand member satisfaction is not the goal. Satisfied members will LEAVE for a better rate. They know the only way to be extremely successful is to focus on their members' success.

  Ordinary credit unions regard "member satisfaction" from their mindset, not from the mindset of the members. The ordinary credit unions don't really know their members and what drives them to or from another financial institution. Rarely are they passionate about their members' results.

- ✓ **Extraordinary Credit Unions** are unique. Whether it's their delivery system, the types of members they serve, the types of products they sell, or the special touches of their member service . . . they clearly define themselves as different and their members know it.

  Ordinary credit unions that look and act like their competitors can count on one thing — competing on price. That game can't be won.

- ✓ **Extraordinary Credit Unions** understand that service is a game of the heart. The greats are focused on passion. They only hire people who are on a "Mission from God." Financial services can be learned. Passion cannot.

  Leaders of average financial institutions think it's a game of the head. Although the intellectual game must be played, it's NOT the turf where the game is won.

- ✓ **Extraordinary Credit Unions** believe that employees come first. Just like Southwest Airlines, the extraordinary hire the best, pay them well, train them incessantly, celebrate joyously, create a sense of play, and have a "get-it-done" attitude. Great performance is generated from a child-like sense of play and a rigorous obsession with constantly improving their staff.

One of the first conversations I have with CEOs of average credit unions is, "It doesn't look like anyone is having any fun out there."

✓ **Extraordinary Credit Unions** develop systems for the areas they define to be important for success. From sales to referrals to member retention systems, they know that what they systemize gets done. Aristotle said, "We are what we repeatedly do." Excellence, then, is not an act, but a habit.

Ordinary credit unions have systems, but they are focused on operational activity. There are no systems for sales, service, and marketing activities. And, if they start a system but their people don't comply, they ignore it and make excuses for it.

✓ **Extraordinary Credit Unions** know their values and live them consistently. Their employees know what they stand for. They pass on opportunities for short-term gain that could impact their long-term plan because they know who they are. They are motivated by making a difference.

Sixty percent of American households are one paycheck away from bankruptcy and eighty percent have a net worth of less than $75,000. And yet, by coaching our members to pay themselves first with a minimal amount of savings, most can accomplish financial independence. The financial services industry has let down its members by being transactional when they needed us to coach them about how to be smarter with their money. Extraordinary financial institutions are motivated by the differences they make in their members' lives.

✓ **Extraordinary Credit Unions** develop a brilliant strategy they are passionate about. They think through how they will deploy their resources for the best possible good. Strategic planning isn't something that is done for regulators. It is a powerful exercise that guides their daily activities and is devoid of "fluff." It spells out the **how**.

After reviewing hundreds of strategic plans by our financial services clients, it is obvious that most are devoid of any strategy. They have goals. They have tactics. But strategy is never addressed. They don't know how to get there . . . only that they should get there. Clicking their heels and hoping they get to Kansas doesn't work for them.

✓ **Extraordinary Credit Unions** understand that when they are evangelists on a mission to convince their employees to give their members something great, growth can't help but follow. As can be seen, culture DRIVES growth.

The ordinary think that reworking the budget one more time will give them what they want. The answer is never in the budget. Growth is not made by slaving over the budget. Not knowing where they come from, the ordinary focus here.

✓ **Extraordinary Credit Unions** know in order to win, they have to be creative and try many different things their competitors didn't think of yet . . . and they do. They constantly try new products, new service approaches, and new targeted marketing tactics. They know that to have the big wins, they need to encourage trying many things . . . and allowing failures.

The ordinary are creatively constipated. They do what they have always done whether it works well or not. They look to other financial institutions for ideas — typically not the place to go for great ideas.

✓ **Extraordinary Credit Unions** focus on their current members. It costs seven times more to get a new member than to do more business with an existing member. A two-percent increase in retention creates an operational cost decrease of 16 percent. Therefore, they aren't transactional. They don't violate their members by selling to them. They coach members how to buy from them. They build trust that this is the place to come for direction on all their financial decisions.

The ordinary focus on getting new members, and they neglect existing members. They are transactional. They have sales campaigns for certain products, causing a monthly blip in the number of credit cards sold that month . . . only to return to the previous level immediately after the campaign. They violate their members by selling to them.

- ✓ **Extraordinary Credit Unions** march to their own beat . . . and it's the beat the members set for them. As the *Wall Street Journal* says of Commerce Bank, a bank that's sounding a wake-up call for the rest of the industry:

"Let's face it: Almost no one likes financial institutions. If it isn't the fees, it's the long lines or the short hours or the surly tellers.

"Now, walk into any branch of Commerce Bancorp . . . Free checking. Free money orders. Weekday teller service from 7:30 in the morning to 8 at night. And branch service with real tellers on weekends and holidays — even a few hours on Sundays."

Every one of their branches looks like every other location right down to the carpeting. Their service is standardized. They hire passion and train employees incessantly about the values for which they stand, and they wouldn't even think of acquiring as a means for growth.

Ordinary credit unions don't pay much attention to what the members are asking for. They tend to pay more attention to what other financial institutions are doing.

- ✓ **Extraordinary Credit Unions** experience a deeper level of truth telling. As best I can tell, the perfect human has not yet been designed. We are all works in progress. For that progress to accelerate, leaders need to create an environment where it's safe to tell the truth. Jim Collins, in his book, *Good to Great*, observed that great companies had management teams that really fought for their ideas, but in a respectful way. They attacked ideas without attacking people. Going beyond that, I find that the best leaders in financial institutions create an atmosphere where all employees and leaders lovingly give input to each other with each other's development as the goal. They hire people who are "coachable" as opposed to those who are offended by feedback.

The ordinary don't deal with issues to consensus. Passive-aggressive infighting is accepted and people aren't standing up for what they believe. Instead, they leave leadership meetings and sabotage the results by playing petty games of "told you so." Issues aren't addressed in productive and healthy ways.

✓ **Extraordinary Credit Unions** have leadership that is committed to being the people they were meant to be. They are "self-improvement" machines. They find their way to improvement has more with how they choose to "be" than what they choose to "do." They understand that work is essential to joy — and that sustainable joy is an inside job.

In ordinary credit unions, very little attention is paid to developing the "whole" person. Training is for skill sets only. Personal development is seen as an unnecessary luxury.

Qualities of the Extraordinary

Bottom line distinction: The extraordinary are brave. They're NOT perfect. They admit their frailties to their associates and invite their help to be better. And, they demand that their people do the same. They sincerely care for the people around them and realize they're in the business of making themselves and their team better people. Good people attract good results.

Learn the Rewards of Being Uncomfortable

This book is intended to make you uncomfortable. The best are always uncomfortable. Change can be encouraged for a lifetime, but nothing compels a person to change more than dissatisfaction gnawing at their soul. It is that feeling of *there must be more* that drives extraordinary performance.

As many of my top-performing clients do, my wish is that you, too, will bring this book and more of my e-mail newsletters (free at www.EmmerichFinancial.com) into your leadership meetings on a weekly or monthly basis and talk of implementation. Ideas are interesting, but execution of those ideas is necessary for results.

These principles are the foundation for the Seven Strategies yet to follow. The strategies are step-by-step blueprints that, with very little effort, enable any financial institution to have great success. I've had clients tell me that by implementing just one of these, they felt it was a "miracle." They couldn't imagine how they could get those kinds of results that quickly. They do work. However, the reason I covered the above principles first is that this foundation must constantly be nourished for these templates to deliver **sustainable** results.

Results are influenced by three things:

Luck, effort, and skill.

Luck can't be influenced.

Effort is an absolute. Nothing great comes without commitment to execute.

And, this book is the template for extraordinary skill.

Extraordinary Credit Unions is about teaching you the principles, processes, and systems to take you from surviving to thriving.

My wish is that you thrive both personally and professionally and experience abundance far beyond monetary gains — that you get a feeling in your heart that your life impacted this world.

Enjoy the ride,

Roxanne Emmerich

Breakthrough to Extraordinary Member Service

Turn Service into Growth by Becoming Obsessed about . . . Member Success!

The foundation for growth is member service. Without extraordinary service, from the MEMBER'S viewpoint, all sales and marketing efforts and all brilliant strategies are only expensive efforts with little return.

Member retention and evangelistic referrals from members is the first effort that each financial institution must master.

While most executives think they deliver great service, the national research from members shows the discrepancy between the financial institution's perception and the members' perception is alarming. My area newspaper just published an article that included a sad statistic about a large local financial institution: One-half of its clients who opened new accounts would close those accounts within six months. This same organization spends an astronomical amount on advertising their **outstanding member service**! As they say in the South, "This dog won't hunt!"

Most of the top-performing credit unions we've researched are adamant about not using the word "sales" in their credit unions. They use the word among managers, but *never* in front of employees. They know that the point is not to "sell." They know to direct employees to take such excellent care of members that they will automatically purchase everything they need at that credit union. Their employees know to convince their members to always come to them first for every financial need. Their members feel like they are taken "under wing," sheltered, protected, counseled, assisted, and properly informed in all of their financial matters — so they don't need to go anywhere else.

"Member Satisfaction" Is for Wimps

You can have members who are satisfied, but they'll leave you for a better rate. The ONLY thing that keeps members is a feeling of assurance that you are focused on their success!

Top-performing credit union managers know that spectacular service will create sales. You should gauge good service by the facts that (1) your members never leave; they always remain loyal to you and thus remain your member; (2) they bring all of their business your way now and in the future; and (3) they tell others about you.

Contrast this strategy to a real-life experience I had several years ago:

The Saga Begins . . .

> It was a beautiful spring Monday morning in Minneapolis. I had just moved my business from another state and had spent the prior week setting up my new office. Now it was time to take care of the logistics. I needed a new financial institution.
>
> Not knowing any of the financial institutions in the area or their reputations, I decided to stop at the one closest to my office. My thought was that the convenience would outweigh any minor differences I might encounter.

When I walked in at 8:02 a.m., it was obvious that I was the only potential customer or client in the financial institution. There was no signage identifying where the new accounts area was. Therefore, I walked to the nearest teller station. It would seem I would get direction there.

As I approached the station, I witnessed what I can best describe as "parts disease." All I saw were scalp parts. All employees had their heads down. No one attempted to make eye contact. As a kid I remember thinking it would come in handy to be invisible at times, but this was ridiculous.

I stopped in front of the teller station. I stood there for some time while the young woman shuffled papers. She never acknowledged my presence. I was completely invisible to her. Because of my move, my time was even more valuable and limited than usual. Thus, I decided to draw attention to myself. After all, I was so close to the teller that she should have heard my breathing.

"Excuse me," I said. (A long pause followed.) "Excuse me, miss. I'm wondering if you could tell me where I might be able to go to open a checking account?" I asked clearly.

Her reply, without even looking up, was, "I'm sorry lady, but I'm just a teller."

"Okay," I said, "But could you tell me where I could open a checking account?" I asked again, trying my best to be pleasant.

"You'll have to sign in at that book over on that table and wait your turn," she answered without looking up.

At this point, the ridiculousness of the situation nearly became comedic. I had to concentrate to keep a straight face. Wait my turn? I was still the only customer or potential customer in the whole place. And *I* didn't "have to" do anything. That's why God invented competition.

By now, I had come to terms with the fact that this wasn't going to be my financial institution, but my curiosity had kicked in and I wanted to stick around and see how bad it could get.

After signing in, I waited "my turn." Employees were laughing about how awful their customers were, gossiping about their coworkers, wasting time, and complaining about what a horrible place it was to work. Yes, they were doing this all within my (their potential new customer's) earshot and line of vision. I was sure they were right about it being a horrible place to work!

This would not be a good place to work or do business.

After another five-minute wait, a young woman closed her *Minneapolis Tribune*, walked over to "the book," crossed off my name, and shouted, "ROXANNE EMMERICH!"

In shock, I looked to my left, to my right, in back of me, in front of me, and finally came to the same conclusion: I was still the only customer-like person in the building!

Deciding to play the game, I walked over to the desk. What followed would have been astonishing if it had not been for the forewarning of preceding events. I would have been a fool if I expected anything other than disaster, and I was not disappointed.

"What do you want?" asked the new accounts person.

"Well, I'm considering opening a checking account," I said with my hand out, which was ignored.

"Okay, please give me your driver's license and social security card."

Clearly, we weren't going to be best friends. She was hardly making any attempt to be friendly. It just kept getting worse. Not only did she not have any interest in my needs or desires, she had no interest in attempting to look like she cared.

Had she been trained and inspired, she could have started with a comment such as a cordial "Hello, I'm _____. What brings you in to us today?" Such a greeting would have created a plethora of opportunities for the financial institution to acquire a new lifelong customer and for me to have a lifelong financial institution that I respected and trusted. I suspect she could have uncovered ten of my needs that would have created a great bond with her financial organization, not to mention creating ten profitable transactions.

Here's How It Should Have Happened:

"What brings you to us today?" the lady asks as she greets me with a smile and a handshake.

"Well, I just moved my business so I need to switch checking accounts," I state.

"Interesting. What kind of business do you have?"

"We work with financial institutions to create systems and mindsets to help our clients become and stay number one in their markets."

"I see. May I ask what prompted the move?"

"Since I travel so often, I need to live in a hub city so I can get home at night."

"Have you moved your home? Do you have a family that moved with you?"

On and on the questions should have come. If this had been the case, I would have opened a business checking account, a personal checking account, an IRA rollover, profit-sharing rollover, direct deposit payroll, a mortgage, and a plethora of other ancillary services. Clearly, that was *never* going to be the case.

The service I received that day turned me away from opening a checking account or doing any other business with that financial institution.

Several years later, I met the CEO of that financial institution at a conference. When I asked him what differentiated his organization from others, he said proudly, "Service!" I suspect I did lasting damage to my tongue that day as I nearly bit it off!

Unfortunately, this type of nightmare service and the leaders, who underestimate the severity of the problem, are not rare enough. While most financial institution CEOs state they stand out in their customer/member service, national surveys clearly show that consumers feel the financial services industry ranks lowest in this area when compared to nearly all other service industries.

Why the discrepancy?

Many managers are too far removed from the problems of their members to understand members' experiences with their credit unions. In fact, the people who call a CEO tend to be those who are either EXTREMELY dissatisfied or those who are extremely delighted.

Your mainstream business comes from all those who fall between these extremes.

How does a credit union management team dramatically improve member service and make sure it is consistent from branch to branch?

Ask the right questions.

Question:

How do you stop preaching member service and eliminate the "do gap" between what you want and what actually happens?

Solution:

Create an ironclad member service strategy and monitor it rigorously.

Example:

> Jan Carlson took over the reins of Scandinavian Air at a time when the airline was suffering an $8 million loss and turned it around to a $71 million profit within one year.
>
> He created a miracle with more than a hope and a prayer or even a little charismatic leadership. He created a strategy that was so airtight it left no room for misinterpretation.
>
> Carlson started his "miracle" by identifying every "Moment of Truth" that each customer encountered. He defined a Moment of Truth as each time a customer had the opportunity to form an impression of the business. He felt that at each of those Moments, a customer would either feel better or worse about Scandinavian Airlines. He felt that if he managed every one of those Moments meticulously, he could create extremely positive impressions consistently, thereby increasing the amount of repeat and referral business.

He identified some of his Moments of Truth as being the cleanliness of the waiting area, the announcements of the pilot, the check-in process, and even the cleanliness of the plane.

For example, Carlson felt that if a customer saw a coffee stain on a tray when it was pulled down from the seat back, then that person's first thought would be, "Oh my goodness, I wonder if they remembered to service the engines."

> **One impression creates concerns for other areas.**

As a frequent traveler on planes, I pray every day that the same person who cleans off those trays isn't the one who services the engines! I think not. But each person's perceptions create his or her reality.

Carlson's point is that passengers are likely to make unreasonable assumptions about whether coffee stains really have anything to do with the area they might worry about. Why? Because the human brain makes those leaps. It is, therefore, very important to manage the perceptions.

The real question is, how do you apply a system that turned a company from a devastating loss to a sensational gain in only one year so you, too, can create such a powerful benefit for your company?

There are nine simple steps which, when implemented, will definitely benefit you immediately and far into the future.

Step #1: Gather Your People Together.

There is a magic that happens when people gather to learn together. Research shows the amount of learning that is actually implemented when someone trains outside your facility is frighteningly close to *zero*.

No matter how good the intentions may be, when people learn something without their peers learning it at the same time it doesn't work as well as when the entire team learns it together. Why? It is a rather daunting task to go back and not only change your own work processes, beliefs, and habits, but show others how to change at the same time. It is simply harder than if all involved are at the same level of commitment to change and have the same tools so they can implement change immediately.

What happens if learning is done by individuals rather than by the whole group? The individuals may implement the new standards for a short period of time, but once they recognize that those with whom they work have not changed, they have the tendency to slip back into their old patterns.

It is very possible to train technical skills with an outside seminar or speaker. This can be very effective because they are individual skills, not group-related activities. However, when it comes to training in the areas of organizational development, it is **critical** to train people together in the same room and at the same time.

There is a powerful phenomenon called peer pressure that can be utilized very effectively to get a group of people to shift at once in the right direction. I saw this happen after doing one "after hours" session. The CEO told me, "I've been doing this for 24 years and if you would have told me you could shift the attitudes so dramatically in one session and make it sustainable, I never would have believed you. What we saw happen here was a miracle."

It's no miracle. When a group gets together in a session and lists all the things they think are examples of horrible member service, their peers gasp at some of the terrible service. The guilty perpetrators who are sitting amongst them are quite confident they can't go back and do those things again. The gig is up.

There is one other reason you want to get your entire group together to create your service strategy. When they create a process, it's their idea. Who can they blame? Who can they fight? Who cannot use their own idea? You're right: They can't resist their own strategy. They can't say, "I don't have time," or "You don't understand," or "Who thought of this anyway?" People who create a strategy will naturally want to follow through with it. Their creative input is on the line. So what do you do when you get them in the room?

Step #2: **List the Moments of Truth.**

Pose the question to your group, "At what specific times or under what circumstances do our members form specific impressions of us?"

They will start to list things like:
- Phone etiquette
- Sales calls
- Greetings
- Rate inquiry calls
- Building appearance
- Attitude and appearance of our people
- Correspondence and statements

- Recovering from a mistake or dissatisfied member
- Loan closings
- Follow-up calls and correspondence for current members

Ask your people to keep listing the times when your members form an impression of you until you think you've exhausted the list.

Step #3: Identify What You *DON'T* Want.

Experience the power of "shock training" — why not try asking your employees to list service violations they've seen elsewhere? This will shock violators into waking up.

Example:

If your employees listed phone etiquette as one of their Moments of Truth, you can then ask the question, "What are examples of some really terrible phone skills?"

Possible Responses:

- When someone doesn't identify oneself
- When a person's voice is depressing and lacking in confidence
- When the phone rings for a long period of time before someone answers
- When you are put on hold without being asked for your permission
- When someone puts you on hold for over 30 seconds

- When someone transfers the call several times before they get it to the right person
- When someone tells you what they CAN'T do
- When someone uses wimpy language like, "I'll try."
- And the list goes on and on

Notice that this technique can be used for any standard your credit union has.

Now realize that already, just by going this far, there are many people in the room who have violated some of these "unmentionable acts." They will probably be extremely careful to never make those mistakes again. The bar has already been raised by watching the disgust on their fellow workers' faces about how awful these violations appear to others.

After they have listed a series of examples, the next step is to set standards around those atrocities so they don't happen in your credit union.

Step #4: Set Your Standards.

The group should, for each Moment of Truth, list quantifiable and measurable standards.

> **Be Specific!**

Don't say esoteric things such as, "Our goal is to have happy members," or "Be good on the phone." Instead, make sure that every standard could be shopped by an outside person. Thus, it would be clear that you either did or did not meet the standard.

Examples:

Standard: Phone

- Pick up the phone by the second or third ring.
- Always start with an acknowledgement, your name, department when appropriate, and an offer to help. For example: "Thank you for calling XYZ. This is Julie. How may I help you?"
- Always use the member's name at least once in the conversation.
- Transfer the call only once and announce the call to the person to whom it is transferred to assure the right person is receiving and accepting the call.
- Use a confident and joyful voice.
- Never say what you cannot do. Instead, say what you **can do**.
  - ✓ Don't say, "I can't have those papers to you until Wednesday."
  - ✓ Instead say, "I can have those papers to you on Wednesday."
- Always give the caller a choice between leaving their message on voice mail or with a person instead of automatically transferring them into voice mail.
- Return phone calls within one hour.
- If the person the caller is looking for is unavailable, offer to help them yourself or ask if they would prefer to leave a message.
- Always ask how else you can help before concluding the call.
- Thank the caller for calling.

Notice that in each case, the standard is quantifiable; callers will be able to measure whether each standard is achieved.

Your employees will perceive the importance of something by the amount of attention you spend designing and following the strategy.

For each Moment of Truth there needs to be quantifiable and measurable standards set by your entire staff at the same time. Resist the temptation to have your management team or CEO set those standards and then pass them down from "on high." It won't work. People are likelier to follow processes for which their input was requested and for which they had some creative license.

The role of management is to raise the bar. As your staff is setting the standards, don't simply challenge them to be just a little better, but coach them on the concept of being EXTRAORDINARY.

When they say something like, "We should answer all phones by the fourth ring, challenge them. Ask, "That might be acceptable member service, but what would we do if we wanted to have EXTRAORDINARY service?" Let them create from there.

Just as the drawers wouldn't balance without a specific strategy and rigorous monitoring, neither can sales nor service function optimally without a specific strategy and system put in place and followed with thorough monitoring.

Step #5: Add Distinguishable Standards that Emphasize Your Uniqueness.

Macaroni Grill, an Italian restaurant chain, has many unique standards that make it distinguishable and impressive compared to its competition. The singing waiter is one of those standards. Another standard that always delights customers is the display of playfulness amidst the somewhat elegant ambiance. The server comes out and signs his or her first name upside down in crayon on the table cover. This helps the customers remember their waiter's name. This ALWAYS happens — no exception.

Macaroni Grill has taken a brand of "be an elegant yet fun environment that is entertaining and comfortable to the customer" and built a system such that every person who ever comes in is shocked to see this crayon come out but is also delighted at how interesting it is.

What unique standards can you implement? Brainstorm this with your employees.

Step #6: Evangelize the Standards with a Flair for the Extreme.

Every human should have at least one convertible in his or her lifetime. I acquired mine several years ago when I went shopping for a car with my highly enthusiastic fourth-grade son. I made an extreme choice of taking a test drive in a blue Saab convertible that looked just adorable. On a beautiful spring day in Minneapolis, with the wind in our hair and the stereo cranked to our favorite hip-hop song, we hadn't driven more than a block when my son, bursting with excitement, looked over at me and said, "Mom, you just HAVE TO HAVE THIS CAR!"

We drove it home that day and didn't think twice about it until winter fell upon us once again. Then it seemed reasonable to assume that a convertible perhaps was not the ideal vehicle in Minneapolis. Actually, a two-ton truck with a snowplow mounted on the front would have been much more practical. But, I have to say, I did love that car, and up until that fateful blue Saab day, I didn't even know that Saab made convertibles.

In fact, up until that day, I had never even noticed a blue Saab convertible anywhere. From that day on, however, I happened to notice them all around Minneapolis. I saw them everywhere.

What was in the background, but still there, suddenly came to the foreground.

That's exactly what needs to happen with your member service standards. They need to be brought to the foreground in the minds of your employees.

How do they get there? You have to set the standards and then broadcast them in a unique and remarkable way. But mainly your employees need to eat, sleep, and breathe them each and every day.

Your credit union's standards need to be posted, printed, included in employee newsletters, and built into performance reviews. They should be mystery shopped. They should be a part of every new employee orientation. And they should be evangelized on a weekly basis. Whatever medium you use to communicate, be sure to always, always, always include those standards.

It's when your standards take on this type of importance that they are visibly brought to the foreground so that your people really believe they should be the focus of every day.

Step #7:   Attain Complete and Total Commitment from Everyone.

The most important part of your meeting is the conclusion. It's the part where the *passion* for being extraordinary and actually doing what you say you are going to do is paramount.
I often tell powerful stories of commitment and situations where people removed their excuses and just did what they said they were going to do. The results? Powerful.

It's critical to look people in the eye and ask for that commitment. They need to declare that they want to be extraordinary.

It's the "throwing the heart over the bar" that makes the impact. No great member service revolution ever happened as a result of an intellectual conversation. It's the passion that moves it forward.

Until you penetrate the core of the issues and spark the desire to perform at that core level, **nothing has really happened!** So your employees will live by the standards, get each of them to commit verbally and/or in writing before they leave the room.

Step #8: Implement Commitments Immediately with High Expectations.

At the very same session where you have your staff list your Moments of Truth and create your standards for each, announce that you expect those standards to be implemented immediately and consistently. Let all your employees know that everyone must not only manage themselves and their consistency, but also coach those around them not to slip.

> The 24-hour rule: If people don't apply what they learned within 24 hours, they will probably never implement it.

Every time I do a session, I recommend that the management team come prepared at the end of the session to announce a **Mystery Shopping Awards Program**. I have them announce it in exactly the following way with excitement and enthusiasm:

Immediately

> Starting tomorrow morning, from the very first call, we expect everyone to be in complete compliance with every one of these standards. To make sure you are, we're going to help you by providing Mystery Shopping so you can see how well you're doing and where you need to improve. The **Mystery Shopping Awards** will be announced at the end of the first week.

First Week

> At the end of each week, we will distribute the Mystery Shopping results and have a celebration. All those receiving a score of a perfect 10 will receive a free movie pass, a $10 bill, or a free breakfast or lunch (or whatever prize management chooses). Each winner's name will go in a hat for the weekly grand prize of a $100 gift certificate to the mall or a day at the spa (or, again, whatever is of perceived value to your employees).

Third Week

> The third week, we will choose from all the names that went in the hat for the ultimate grand prize of a weekend for two at some desired location or a substantial gift certificate.

Only two days into the Mystery Shopping process, one CEO told me, "I don't suppose CEOs are supposed to use language like this, but I'm giddy. My customers are calling me and walking into my office asking, 'What happened here?'"

This is the same CEO whose organization hadn't grown in four years, and he was now telling me they grew deposits five percent in two weeks. Better yet, they discovered it was sustainable when they grew 50 percent in the next six months!

Why did this CEO and so many other clients of ours receive such powerful results without the need for a market study, a top-six consulting firm strategic plan, or even voodoo?

What Transpired to Cause Radical Change?

What happened is that they brought this concept into the foreground with the complete expectation that every employee would follow and maintain the system, and the focus stayed in place long enough so that the employees began to form daily habits of success.

Key to Successful Mystery Shopping

Many service firms offer Mystery Shopping, but many are too slow to deliver the information for it to be meaningful. Many are outrageously priced, thereby limiting the number of shops.

You *don't* want to do that.

> **You want every employee to be shopped each week for three weeks.**

Obviously, there are times when, after many attempts, a few of your people just can't be reached. However, every effort should be made to make sure each person receives feedback on a weekly basis.

Low-Cost Mystery Shopping Do-It-Yourself Kit

You can Mystery Shop by phone yourself. For a downloadable form for Mystery Shopping, visit www.EmmerichFinancial.com. You can simply download this form and hire a bright intern, a stay-at-home mom who understands financial services, members of the seniors' club, or people from one of your locations to shop another location.

The most important thing your shoppers must understand is that they MUST do their job on time so the results are delivered on time. This shows employees that you, too, are rigorous about your systems.

An Added Benefit: Implementing Mystery Shopping also makes your shoppers aware that you are concerned about providing the best member service possible. By hiring people in the community, you may easily expand your member base and spread word of mouth — a two-for-one deal!

Step # 9: Never Ever Drop Member Service into the Background.

Follow up and follow through: Our research with financial institutions shows that, after three weeks of Mystery Shopping, the average employee score improves from 4.6 the first week to over 9 by the third week.

Why?

Because by you sustaining the process, your employees realize it isn't going to go away. This isn't another one of those "This, too, shall pass" programs.

I also remind management teams that their most important job during this time is to coach. Their job is to hand deliver each shop and no matter what the score is, congratulate the employee on what he or she did right and say,

> "I see you received 5 out of 10. Next week I know you can make a 10. Is there any help you need from me to make sure you receive consistent 10s from now on?"

Notice that the psychological approach is specific and based on some extremely valuable principles:

- Make the person feel good about what was done right.
- Explain that your expectations are extremely high.
- Let employees know that *you* know they can meet or exceed the expectations.
- Offer to help without taking away their responsibility.
- Let them know you haven't given up.

> **What is expected must be inspected!**

After the initial three-week campaign to bring member service to a whole new level, all of your communication, shopping, and focus must be centered on member service. If this is not true, then you can expect member service quality to drop off.

How do you prevent this drop-off?

Let your staff know that there will be intermittent Mystery Shopping that will not be announced. Those shops must always count for something. You certainly want those shops to be a part of performance reviews as well as continued celebrations and high performance campaigns.

Create a great empire and build your fortress around it for protection. Most importantly, make sure the flag of communicating the standards is never lowered.

For information on how to maximize this process, call our office at 1-800-236-5885 and ask for a FREE special report on member service strategies.

(Example sheet)

Moments of Truth

Have participants list their own Moments of Truth. Here are some suggestions you won't want to miss:

- Phone calls
- Correspondence
- Greetings
- Loan applications
- Statements
- Building appearance
- Bookkeeping inquiries
- Cleanliness of waiting areas
- Voice mail
- Processing times
- New account openings
- Transaction processing
- Pricing inquiries
- Signage
- Loan closings
- Product presentations

Phone Standards

(Use only as a guide and have participants come up with standards so they OWN them.)

- Pick up phone by second or third ring.
- Always offer your name.
- Greet with "Thank you for calling (name of institution). This is (your name). How may I help you?"
- Always thank the member for calling.
- Ask what else you can help the member with.
- Project confidence and competence.
- Ask permission before putting someone on hold, and wait for an answer.
- Return phone calls within one hour.
- Offer your name when you place an outbound call.
- Transfer each call only once.
- Never say what you can't do; always say what you can do.
- Use the member's name at least once in each call.
- Update your voice mail daily.

Correspondence Standards

- Similar font on all outgoing correspondence.
- Thank you card sent out within 24 hours of new account opening.
- Letter to potential members within 2 days of initial call.
- Statements understandable and neatly printed.
- Statements out within 24 hours of cycle.
- Quarterly newsletter to all members.
- Follow-up call within 3 days of opening new account.
- Logo on all marketing materials and letterhead.
- Laser printer for all letters.
- All new-account forms professionally printed.

Make a "Commitment to You" of 10 items

Work on 25 — that will make us extraordinary. (every day)

Moment of Truth

_____

Quantifiable Standards:

1. _____
2. _____
3. _____
4. _____
5. _____
6. _____
7. _____

Moment of Truth

_____

Quantifiable Standards:

1. _____
2. _____
3. _____
4. _____
5. _____
6. _____
7. _____

Moment of Truth

_____

Quantifiable Standards:

1. _____
2. _____
3. _____
4. _____
5. _____
6. _____
7. _____

Moment of Truth

_____

Quantifiable Standards:

1. _____
2. _____
3. _____
4. _____
5. _____
6. _____
7. _____

Moment of Truth

_____

Quantifiable Standards:

1. _____
2. _____
3. _____
4. _____
5. _____
6. _____
7. _____

Moment of Truth

_____

Quantifiable Standards:

1. _____
2. _____
3. _____
4. _____
5. _____
6. _____
7. _____

Moment of Truth

_____

Quantifiable Standards:

1. _____
2. _____
3. _____
4. _____
5. _____
6. _____
7. _____

Moment of Truth

_____

Quantifiable Standards:

1. _____
2. _____
3. _____
4. _____
5. _____
6. _____
7. _____

Moment of Truth
_____

Quantifiable Standards:

1. _____
2. _____
3. _____
4. _____
5. _____
6. _____
7. _____

Moment of Truth
_____

Quantifiable Standards:

1. _____
2. _____
3. _____
4. _____
5. _____
6. _____
7. _____

Moment of Truth

_____

Quantifiable Standards:

1. _____
2. _____
3. _____
4. _____
5. _____
6. _____
7. _____

Moment of Truth

_____

Quantifiable Standards:

1. _____
2. _____
3. _____
4. _____
5. _____
6. _____
7. _____

Summary

The point of this chapter is to turn your member service into a center for continued business with your existing members.

When service is great enough, when it is extraordinary, then sales become automatic. When service is substandard, then members disappear to more service-oriented institutions.

Look at your credit union from the eyes of your members and potential members. What do they see, hear, and feel about your credit union? Determine how you can improve this perception. Most credit union managers and CEOs never meet the average member.

The Ultimate Solution to Great Member Service: Create an ironclad member service strategy and monitor it rigorously. Take the following nine simple steps that will benefit you immediately and way into the future.

Step #1:	Gather Your People Together.
Step #2:	List the Moments of Truth.
Step #3:	Identify What You *DON'T* Want.
Step #4:	Set Your Standards.
Step #5:	Add Distinguishable Standards that Emphasize Your Uniqueness.
Step #6:	Evangelize the Standards with a Flair for the Extreme.
Step #7:	Attain Complete and Total Commitment from Everyone.
Step #8:	Implement Commitments Immediately with High Expectations.

> **The 24-hour Rule:** If people don't apply what they have learned within 24 hours, they will probably never implement it.

Step # 9: Never Ever Drop Member Service into the Background

Identify your **Moments of Truth** and constantly look for ways to create the impressions you want with potential and existing members.

Action Plan for Implementing Strategies in Chapter 1

Action to Take	Responsible Person	Results	Start Date	Target Date

Benefits

2 Breakthrough Vision to Outstanding Success

Vision It Possible:

Create a Compelling Direction That Enrolls People's Hearts, Minds, and Souls

Imagine this scenario:

> A credit union CEO holds a quick meeting with the tellers and says, "Okay everyone, thanks for all you do. This year our ROA was 1.0. Next year, our ROA goal is 1.2. So, good luck and go make great things happen!"
>
> The next day, NOTHING changes. The next year, with luck, the ROA will be 1.0.
>
> This CEO has no idea how to get her people's hearts, minds, and souls engaged in doing what needs to be done for results to improve.

And then, of course there's the strategic-planning process . . .

Here's the scene:

It's time for the annual strategic-planning retreat. The hotel conference room is booked. The agenda is set. The board members and upper management check in, all wearing the required strategic-planning uniform: khakis.

The somewhat boring, slightly balding facilitator, complete with a dusty MBA, begins the process by telling the attendees it's time to revisit their mission statement. Five hours later, after a buildup of anxiety and four large carafes of coffee, the final mission statement is declared: "To be a leading provider of financial services, with outstanding member service, and high quality products" — or something highly unique like that.

Whew! Victory is declared. Finally, a restroom break is allowed. With jittery hands and hearts from an overdose of caffeine, the attendees walk down the hallway with a crooked smile on their faces, knowing their cover smiles aren't reflective of what's really going on in their hearts.

They know something is wrong. They just don't know what it is — until the following week when they write up the plan and deliver it to their employees, who jump with joy as they declare, "Thank goodness we have a direction and vision that inspires us." Or not!

Again, hearts, minds, and souls are not engaged.

Out-of-Date Model Gets Out-of-Date Results!

The reality is, the strategic-planning model of the 1970s is a bankrupt model that continues to show up in most boardrooms. This happens because of a lack of understanding about what else can be done. Not knowing how to improve on the model, most groups just follow the system. A year later, they are then extremely shocked when they realize how little was accomplished and how short they fell in driving the necessary change of behavior to take their organization to the greater destination they had envisioned.

Let's dissect what went wrong.

Begin by Considering the Built-in "NO" Response:

> It would benefit all of us to remember what it was like to raise a two-year-old child. The newborn comes into life unencumbered by social norms. There is no desire to be acceptable. The truth, as the child sees it, rules!
>
> What is the favorite word of a two-year-old? "NO." And we as adults are simply highly socialized two-year-olds.
>
> When people bring us their ideas to implement, we manage to come up with a list of highly socialized responses to their suggestions. Those words are repeated in businesses every day:
>
> "I'm sorry. I'm just too busy."
>
> "I have other initiatives ahead of that one. I'll have to see."

"I'll try."

What they're really saying in their acceptable learned responses is exactly what they would say if they were two years old: "NO!"

When we go away for a few days at a retreat to set direction or close our office doors to create our strategy, we emerge to deliver it to the "underlings" who had no opportunity for input. Then, we ask them to implement OUR ideas as if they were theirs. The only natural response they have is to resist and declare it to be lunacy — in the most socialized way they can think of, of course. They say, "NO!"

So what do you do instead?

Do What It Takes to Get a "YES!" Response:

Involve absolutely as many people within your organization as humanly possible and hold their advice to be important and powerful. That doesn't necessarily mean they all get in the room together. It does mean, however, that you survey them.

- ✓ Ask your employees what they want.
- ✓ Ask them to give you the number one reason members choose you over others.
- ✓ Find out what opportunities your people see for your organization.
- ✓ Find out what they consider to be your competitors' vulnerabilities.
- ✓ Ask them what new trends they think your members may experience and what product and service offerings they think will be needed in response to those trends, and so on.

Take a Lesson from Ford:

> On the other hand, having the entire staff in the room at one time, if at all possible, can be one of the most amazing strategies ever developed. Ford Motor Company had a dramatic turnaround years ago when they brought hundreds of employees into a large room for days and had them form groups to brainstorm best practices and strategies for overcoming obstacles. Not only did the ideas they offered make an impact, but absolutely EVERY employee in that meeting felt he or she was 100 percent personally accountable for turning that company around when those strategies were implemented. They OWNED the result. They OWNED the direction. And they just plain CARED a whole lot more.

If I had to limit all of my advice for CEOs of financial institutions to one thing, it would be to understand that **culture drives growth . . .**

> **When emphasis is placed on enrolling the hearts, minds, and souls of your employees in helping your members, profitability can't help but grow!**

Unfortunately, most leaders spend far too little time managing their most important asset — their people.

It's easy to consume their energies in management functions instead of leadership functions. For example, budgeting becomes a focus — with little understanding that the people really drive what happens in the budget, and just saying it's "so" won't necessarily make it "so."

The Key: A Successful Meeting Mix

When developing sessions during which your people create and own a vision, make sure to involve a good cross section of your employees.

At a recent strategy meeting that I facilitated, the woman who coordinated the institution's seniors' program had some of the best strategy suggestions in the room — better than those of any of the board members and senior executives. She, more than any other person in that meeting, rolled up her sleeves every day and really talked with the elderly members, who were thankful that someone asked. She knew exactly what they were asking for, why they left competing institutions, what the buzz was around town about her institution and its competitors, and what future products would be in demand if they were to be developed.

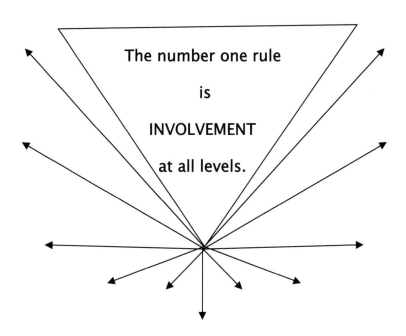

Then what?

Use Art, Not Just Science

Realize that leading an organization is much more an art than a science. You can run budgets all day long, but the proof is in the pudding: Can you get your people to meet those budgets? Can you motivate your people to give everything they've got to make it happen?

History of "No Strategy" = "No Involvement"

Although most of our clientele are high performing, fast-growth financial institutions, my firm occasionally works with a financial institution that is committed to turning itself around from a place of stagnation. Recently, we worked with such an institution — struggling to grow, struggling to get results, struggling to stand out among its competitors.

When I asked for a copy of their strategic plan, I saw a list of goals regarding ROA, ROE, growth projections, loan quality, and so on. Yet, devoid from that strategic plan was any strategy! And unfortunately, that's not a rare occurrence.

There was no direction about how the institution might make its goals happen. No thought was given to differentiation, marketing strategies, positioning, or any of the things that could give the institution any guidance regarding how to get where it said it wanted to go.

Goals were set along with budgets — but no strategy was declared.

In fact, in reviewing hundreds of strategic plans for financial institutions, I've noticed that . . .

Strategy Tends to Be Missing from Almost All of Them!

So, how do you enroll the spirits of those you will need to accomplish your vision?

> **Start with a VISION STATEMENT—**
> *begin with the end in mind.*

Mission statements are almost worthless. They tend to feel like rhetoric and create a "yeah right, whatever" response from most associates.

Your employees have seen them all before. Mission statements are plastered on the walls of almost every business. They're big. They're abstract. They're weak. They lack concreteness. And no one really believes that they matter.

An Example of an Ineffective Mission Statement:

On a recent shopping trip to an office supply store, I spent 10 frustrating minutes looking for something I was sure they would have. I just couldn't understand their logic for the placement of it; thus, I couldn't find it.

After a buildup of frustration, I decided to work smarter and find an associate who could direct me to where the item might be. After five minutes of scouring the store for a human, I finally came upon a person who was counting inventory.

Interestingly, she sat directly below a sign that listed the store's mission statement:

> We at *What a Joke Office Supply Company* intend to be a leading provider of office supplies. Through world-class, prompt and friendly customer service we will maximize our profits to our shareholders.

That was only the first of four paragraphs. Let's just say that had the chains holding that whopper of a mission statement sign broken, it would have split the head of some unlucky customer.

So, now knowing I could expect **"great customer service,"** I embarked upon interrupting the 60ish and stoic gray-haired woman counting inventory. I asked, "Where would I find the clear plastic trays that hold files vertically?"

Perhaps I had some lunch on my face. She looked at me like I was the stupidest being that had ever walked and breathed at the same time. She scowled as she replied, "Listen, can't you see I'm doing inventory? You'll have to find someone else."

My mind flashed to the name of a buddy who is a good therapist. I would have liked to share his number with this woman regarding her anger issues . . . or perhaps *I* should be the one to see a therapist, because my next response was like putting my head in the lion's mouth, expecting, naively, a different result:

"I can see you're busy with inventory. However, I am in a rush to get to an appointment and I know your store carries these because we've purchased them here before. Can you at least direct me to the correct aisle so I can narrow my search?"

It was clear from the look on her face that things were about to get worse.

"Listen, I check people out and I do inventory. I don't put out the stock. I don't know where they put things here. They don't tell me anything. You'll just have to figure it out yourself."

Okay then. You're probably thinking what I thought: "Funny thing she happens to be working under that sign and has never read the darn thing."

So, declaring myself as having an I.Q. over 100, I did the only thing I could do to maintain any self-respect. I left.

Although I've never re-entered that store, I have also never forgotten it. What a vivid example of how a mission statement (a business practice we all consider the only way to start a strategic plan) can be so clearly ineffective.

The problem is that this was not the exception. Mission statements rarely have any positive impact — and they probably never will. But ***vision statements*** do.

Vision Statement

A vision is a clear picture of what happens when you live your values in an extraordinary way.

Your vision is not for the world — it is for your people. It is to get them aligned in a common direction that inspires their work.

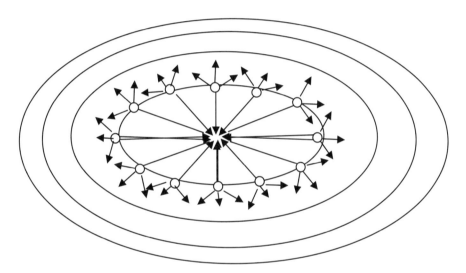

Internal vision, when captured by each individual, creates a ripple effect that goes out to the world and compounds the results!

The Moon Vision:

John F. Kennedy had a vision: **"Put a man on the moon by the end of the decade."** At the time he came up with that vision, we know in retrospect that we had only 15 percent of the information we needed to accomplish it. Yet, in our hearts, minds, and souls, we were compelled to let nothing get in the way.

The Computer Vision:

Bill Gates had a vision: **"To put a computer on every desk in America."** Funny thing was, Bill Gates never made computers. What was he really saying? In mission statement lingo it would have sounded like, "To be a leading provider of software with a high level of innovation, good customer service, high quality products, and an above-average rate of return to our stakeholders."

Had Gates pronounced his vision in these mission statement terms, it's clear the chances of it happening would have been slim to none. Whether you're from the "love Bill" or "hate Bill" camp, you have to give the guy credit for knowing the ART of leading people to create amazing things by enrolling them in wanting to make a difference through their work.

The amazing part is that Microsoft never even made computers! It was about making the world a better place.

High-performance people want to be a part of making a difference. Mediocre performers want a job and a paycheck.

Vision Is the Difference. Let's face it. People don't call home declaring, "Hey honey, today I provided above-average member service." Or, "Wow, babe, I couldn't wait until tonight to let you know that I think we're going to have an above-average return on equity this year!" They call home when they "kicked butt and took names" — they accomplished something amazing that made a difference. It is that focus on making an extraordinary difference that both attracts super achievers and guides the excellence of their work, thereby driving growth and extraordinary results.

Creating Your Vision

Three elements make up a great vision statement.

First: A Vision Statement Is Short with Powerful, Specific Language.

If your vision statement goes beyond one sentence or doesn't read like something a 4th grader would say, it is not going to compel great behavior.

Bold Vision Model:

> When living in Wisconsin over a decade ago, I was asked to be an advisor to Wisconsin's then Governor Tommy Thompson. He put together for the state government the highest ranked task force in 28 years and gave us the role of "creating a bold new direction for state government." I know, I know. It was a little like being asked to leap over a tall building in a single bound. However, this group of fourteen CEOs from some of the largest organizations in

the state, along with a few legislators, met every two weeks for two years to explore how to make it possible.

I was curious to learn what it was about state government that took the life out of so many members of its workforce.

I called one of the lowest-performing departments within state government to do some research on why they seemed to be so ineffective. A not so pleasant, but clearly tenured, employee answered the phone.
I began, "Hi, I'm doing some research, and I'm curious if you could tell me what the mission statement is for your division."

Without any explanation, the phone went quiet. I waited, and someone else picked up the phone. After I asked the same question, the phone went quiet again.

This happened six times until finally a young man picked up the phone and, like a tape recorder having its "play" button hit yet again, I repeated my request.

This time the response was different. He was thrilled. He explained to me that his sole job was to write mission and vision statements for his department.

Hmmm, I thought, not a good sign.

Then he read it. The mission statement was three pages long!

As he finished reading the mission statement, he told me that he had written mission statements for all of the divisions within the department and was curious if I wanted to hear those as well. No thank you. I'd rather have a root canal. Hearing just one was painful enough.

What is the reason for lack of vision?

Although this certainly wasn't the only cause for the lack of joy expressed in that administrative building that day, it brought up a great point: No one knew the mission. No one even knew how to find the mission statement. Moreover, even if they could discover this little treasure, they sure weren't going to remember a word — and they behaved as such.

The Magic Formula:

First: Your vision statement must be short to be effective. One short sentence with fourth-grade language is the magic formula.

Those few words must be **POWERFUL** and **SPECIFIC.** People perform at their language level. If someone says, "I'll have that to you by next Tuesday at 10 a.m.," chances are good you'll see it by then. If, on the other hand, that same person says, "I'll try to see if I can get those to you by Tuesday," you can almost be assured it won't happen then.

It works the same way with vision statements. When esoteric language like "world-class provider" is used, what exactly does that mean? How do you know when you've arrived?

On the other hand, when Nordstrom says, "Every customer comes back asking for a sales associate by name," that clearly sets a standard. Nordstrom employees understand that their job is to create a helpful buying relationship that not only causes them to be remembered, but one that causes the customer to take the extra step of asking for them by name.

Second: A Vision Statement Is Visual!

Can you see a man on the moon? I think we all conjure up an image of what that looks like when we hear the words. Can you see a computer on every desk in America? That one seems easy enough to visualize.

The mind is attracted to pictures, and we feel compelled to move toward those pictures. The value of these mental images is that they are strong and, without exception, seem real. They just are. There's no "iffyness" in them. It's quite clear what a computer on every desk looks like. It just exists. However, a "leading provider of operating system software" leaves plenty of room for ambiguity and wiggling.

Stephen Covey told his son, **"I want the lawn green and clean."** There was no need to micromanage. The clear picture of the end result was painted, leaving no need to micromanage and tell him how often to mow, weed, or fertilize.

Third and Most Important: A Vision Statement Must Be of Service to Others.

Roots of Depression

The high rate of depression in America is alarming. Although chemical imbalances are clearly one culprit that can't be ignored, the alarming growth of this disease begs the question: What feeds this growing state of depression in so many Americans and what is the source of this disease that seems to cause so much loss of will and passion for life?

Although I believe I've never really experienced chronic depression, I've certainly had a few days where I was in a funk and clearly depressed. When I reflect on those days, the one thing I know for sure is where I focused my attention: me, poor miserable me! Nobody appreciates me. Nobody cares about me. Woe is me!

I've asked hundreds of people about this scenario and have found that, without exception, when people are depressed, their focus is internal. It's hard to have a "pity party" when you're out making the world a better place.

Self-centeredness vs. Selflessness

The same thing happens in organizations. The high rate of pettiness within organizations is strongly correlated to how clearly focused the organization is on itself. High-performing companies just don't have the time for self-centeredness. They are powerfully focused on the difference their work makes. They don't have time to whine in a break room. They're up to a bigger game. Interdepartmental strife and whining about someone receiving something in one department and not in another and other such pettiness is almost nonexistent.

There seems to be a correlation: The higher the level of pettiness, the less clear the vision and the more inwardly focused the company tends to be.

> **Bottom line: A vision must focus on making a difference in the world.**

Let's look at a few examples of some excellent vision statements.

Nordstrom's Vision: *[handwritten: We will be the lender for every member's auto loan.]*

> **Every customer will come back asking for a sales associate by name.**

Great one! They could have fouled up this vision with rhetoric that said, "world-class customer service" or "a leading provider of high-end retail clothing and accessories."

They could have cluttered it with esoteric language so no sales associates would have to be accountable. But when you say "every customer," that means, well, every customer.

That means, as an employee, you NEVER just do a transaction. You MUST always find out the customer's name, find out things about them, get their phone number, call them with helpful suggestions, remember their children's names and clothing needs. Those are just a few examples of what is required to create a relationship where the customer asks for you by name.

For Nordstrom, the job isn't just to have good customer service. The job is to make sure EVERY single customer comes back and asks for their sales associate by name.

There's Power in That Vision

While cutting through Nordstrom to get to another store, a sales associate said, "Hi, Roxanne, how are you doing?"

EXTRAORDINARY CREDIT UNIONS

I had not shopped in Nordstrom for several years, yet this lady remembered my name. I was shocked. She continued, "How did that yellow jacket work for that picture you were having taken?" and "How's that cute son of yours doing in baseball?"

Okay, that one did it.

I spent an unbelievable amount of money that day with Nadine. And I never made it to that other store where I had intended to shop.

Based on experience, it looks like Nordstrom's vision works.

Motel Chain Vision Model:

A motel chain I worked with developed a solid vision:

"A head in every bed every night."

No room for mistakes here. By describing an ambitious outcome, this vision statement implicitly says many things: rooms should be immaculate, beds should be made with precision, check-in procedures should be quick and friendly, staff members should be motivating guests to come back again and again — and more.

Financial Services Vision Models:

Several financial institutions I worked with came up with some excellent visions that inspired dramatically improved performance from their people almost immediately.

"Every member retires with financial independence."

This one really set the tone. Suddenly the tellers knew their job wasn't just to do transactions or to "sell." Their job was to look for ways in every transaction to help members financially. This new outlook made quite a significant impact on both the members and the financial institution. Suddenly instead of having to "sell" things, the tellers were helping people buy what they needed — and they felt good about it.

"Every member trusts us with all their financial business and stays with us for life."

Extremely powerful! Unlike most financial institutions that have one or two accounts with each member, this financial institution knew the power of taking its membership completely under their protection. Not only did the members thrive, but the relationship was far more beneficial for both.

"Every member will refer at least three people each year."

You could harp all day long about the value of member service, but when you focus on operating in such a way that you motivate members to risk waving your flag above their house, it means you've got to rise to a whole different level of service. It's especially powerful when the CEO repeats it incessantly and keeps asking people what they need to do differently for each transaction to get members to refer three others.

Overcome Preprogrammed Thinking

Since most people have been inundated with marketing messages all of their lives, most of your staff will come up with marketing slogans when asked to develop a vision. It's hard to think outside the box.

It's important to remember that a vision is not for the market. A vision is for your internal staff to define what extraordinary looks like. It provides the bull's eye.

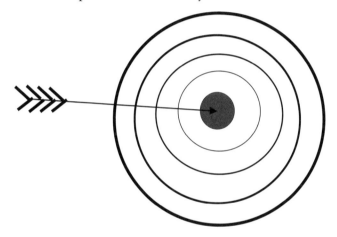

When you and everyone in your organization are on target, you enrich the world around you.

A vision is not a marketing slogan. It's not cute. It doesn't rhyme. It doesn't have multiple interpretations or metaphors or acronyms or alliterations. It's simply a clear picture of what naturally occurs when you live your values in an extraordinary way.

Summary
Three-Step Process to Develop Your Vision Statement

So how do you develop a vision that shifts the mindset of your people to elevate their performance?

1. List Your Driving Values

Start by listing a few values that you most stand for. Don't make a list of ten or twenty, but a short list of two or three that are your driving values. Take only a few minutes to do this. Then ask the following question over and over again until you arrive at a profound picture of an end result.

2. Ask the key question: "If we lived these values in an extraordinary way, what would happen?"

The temptation to say something trite will be overwhelming. So your people will probably say things like, "All of our members are happy."

3. Take It Deeper

When participants give trite answers, simply smile and press on with, "And if that happened, what would happen? And if that happened, what would happen? And if that happened, what would happen?" Use the legendary Deming method of achieving quality answers by asking the question over and over. The third, fourth or fifth response will produce the real answer.

EXTRAORDINARY CREDIT UNIONS

If you're not getting good answers, you're probably not repeating that question, "If that happened, what would happen?" often enough.

Check Your Language

Is the language in your vision strong? Wimpy language produces wimpy results. If you are not specific, then you will not get it done. There is a big difference between "I'll try" and "I'll do." Make your language the DO type.

Don't leave room for ambiguities or ways for even your weakest employee to weasel out. There are commitments and there are excuses. If your vision is not a commitment, then you are allowing excuses.

Don't use corporate jargon. When you say such things as "world-class," realize you haven't said anything of substance and have only created as much rope as is necessary for your people to hang themselves. Rhetoric (such as, "world-class" and "leading provider") is the basis of visions from leaders who are unwilling to really stand for something and figure out how to get there. Because you can't ever know exactly when you are "world-class," your people have no real expectation of arriving there. Some, in fact, would see mediocre performance as "world-class" and think they have arrived when, in fact, they are no where near where they need to be.

Keep Your People in Mind

Your vision statement is for your employees. It is not your marketing slogan, nor is it an external communication. It is your "true north" to get your most important asset, your people, all aligned and rowing toward the same destination, and it gives them the inspiration to get there.

Action Plan for Implementing Strategies in Chapter 2

Action to Take	Responsible Person	Results	Start Date	Target Date

Benefits

3 Breakthrough to Number One Positioning

A credit union is a credit union is a credit union…or is it? If you look like all of your competitors, then your only competition tool is price — and that's a game you can't win.

Positioning
How Do You Wish to Be Perceived to Attract Planned Growth?

In preparation for each speech I give (and I've given almost 200 to groups of financial institution CEOs and directors), I always interview at least 10 and sometimes 100 CEOs. One question I ask repeatedly is:

"What makes your financial institution stand out?"

To that question, I've received only two replies. Over 90 percent of CEOs look at me with inspired expressions on their faces and say, "Service." The other few look at me with glossed-over eyes and say, "I don't know."

Of the two answers, the second one actually is more enlightened. Service never has been and never will be a brand. Although service is absolutely essential to the long-term results of your credit union, it is *never* a position you want to hang your hat on. The financial institutions that do a good job of differentiating themselves are about as rare as straight A's on the entire football team's report cards. Although it happens occasionally, it would come as a pleasant but quite unexpected surprise.

If you are suffering from insomnia, just watch financial service institutions advertisements on television, as they all sound alike and give no reason for you to stay awake, much less take action.

What are the differences between "position," "positioning statement," and "unique-selling proposition?"

Position and *positioning statement* are not the same. As Harry Beckwith states so well in his book *Selling the Invisible*:

> A **position** (or statement of position) is a coldhearted, no-nonsense statement of how you are perceived in the minds of your prospects.

> A **positioning statement**, by contrast, expresses how you wish to be perceived. It is the core message you want to deliver in every medium.

Don't confuse the two. Remember that your organization cannot position itself. Rather, your position is determined by how the market perceives you. Position is a measure of reality in the minds of your potential members and members.

You express how you'd like to be perceived through your positioning statement. Your **unique selling proposition** (USP), based on that positioning statement, is the key message you send out to your market that entices them to want your unique benefit.

All of your communications — from your statements to your letters to your print advertising — must be aligned with the position you intend to own.

Your positioning statement should answer these seven key questions:

1. Who are you?
2. What business are you in?
3. What members do you serve?
4. What's most needed by your market?
5. Against whom do you compete?
6. What's different about your business?
7. What unique benefit is derived from your product or services?

The quality of the answers will determine the quality of your future. A wrong answer can cause you to spin your wheels on a lot of low-potential activity. The point is not to be busy. **The point is to have greater growth and make a greater difference for your members.**

> ### Here's a Challenge for You . . .
>
> **Warning:** *Acceptance of this challenge is only for the brave, as you will probably be depressed by the result.*
>
> Bring your entire leadership team together and ask them the preceding seven questions. Record their answers and analyze their differences, similarities and possible values. Throw out the weak, ineffective, vague, and ordinary answers.

You'll probably find very little agreement among your managers' responses to these very basic questions, which are the foundation for creating your positioning statement and USP.

Even more alarming is that the answers to these questions often are misguided and geared toward a focal point of mediocrity that will only ensure you'll work harder with minimal results!

So how can you be sure your entire leadership team has an appropriate and united focus? And how can you get your marketing and communication all going in the same direction and relaying a clear and enticing message to your potential members and members?

After getting over the shock of your organization's lack of direction and substance, start at the beginning.

> ### Another Challenge for You . . .
>
> Get your management team together and write a clear, defensible, differentiated positioning statement. Then create your key message, or **Unique Selling Proposition (USP)**.

This process will take a great deal of deeper-level truth telling and hard work as you strive for consensus. It may, however, be some of the most valuable time you spend. It will help you align everyone and everything in the same direction for a far better result.

Examples to Stimulate Your Thinking:

Many auto manufacturers have done an excellent job of positioning their uniqueness. Others have lost positioning by not paying attention to the importance of their position and subsequently watering down their brands.

The Volvo Position:

When you think of safety, you probably think of Volvo. Why? Because Volvo has done a wonderful job of marketing that positioning in the minds of its clients. It is interesting to note that for many years, some research showed that Saab, NOT Volvo, was the safest car. Yet when consumers were asked for an example of the safest car, they suggested Volvo over Saab.

The Cadillac Position: Luxury
The Mercedes Position: Engineering
The BMW Position: "Fun to Drive"
The Volkswagen Beetle Position: Reverse Snob

Volkswagen, in its revival of the Beetle, has taken a no-nonsense, practical approach, much like the Beetle itself. What a statement, plus a marketplace with its built in clientele: those who had a VW Beetle in their youth!

What's interesting about all the positioning of these auto manufacturers? The public's perceptions are **exactly** as the companies' marketing departments intended. For example, Mercedes is not seen as a high-end, quality engineered vehicle in Europe as it is here in the United States. In fact, most of the world thinks of Mercedes as being "just a car." However, because of specific marketing strategies, Mercedes was able to appeal to an American value of status symbols and own the position of the car that merits a call to mom: "See mom, I did make something of myself!"

Bank of America Model:

> Bank of America did a wonderful job staking a claim with its unique selling proposition during the 2002 Winter Olympics. With a skier falling head over tail down a ski slope, an announcer claimed:
>
> > **"There are some things we don't do very well, but we *have* figured out how to eliminate 80 percent of the up-front paperwork involved in mortgages."**
>
> Even though many financial services institutions had done exactly the same thing, Bank of America now owned a brilliant position in the consumer's mind. If you were a busy person in need of a mortgage, what are the chances that Bank of America would be the first place you'd want to call?
>
> **What's the magic formula?**
> Bank of America staked a claim with a guarantee that mattered to the consumer!

EXTRAORDINARY CREDIT UNIONS

What made this work?

- **It sounded *tangible*.** They didn't say, "We're the friendly bank" or "Your hometown bank" or "Where customers matter" (or other rhetorical slogans that ineffective marketing companies pitch to financial institutions with no under-standing of what really works). They said, "We eliminate 80 percent of the up-front paperwork." It sounded real. It was believable. The number made it concrete.

- **It implied a *guarantee*.** The implied difference between someone who says, "I'll try to have the paperwork to you by sometime next week" and someone who says, "My name is Tom, and I will have the papers to you by 1 p.m. on Tuesday" is huge. The second person's language is strong and firm, which implies a guarantee. Most financial institutions have wimpy marketing messages that fall on deaf ears and thus miss opportunities for powerful results.

- **Most importantly, it *mattered* to the consumer.** Many financial services institutions continue to focus their lead marketing messages on Internet services, while consumer research by American Research Group basically proved that less than 15 percent care!

What Bank of America tapped into was the fact that people DO care about saving time — especially during the extremely busy experience of moving a residence. In fact, most people complain of scarcity of time far more than they complain of scarcity of money.

These three elements are essential in a powerful USP. So how do you stake your claim in such a way that it makes you stand out from your competitors and compels your potential members, as well as your competitors' clients, to come to you and not them?

I have had the luxury of working with hundreds of financial organizations and have been able to benchmark the good practices that create great results versus those that result in further struggling. One thing is clear across the board:

> *We can never see things clearly when they revolve around our own issues.*

Emotions get in the way of making good decisions. The forest can't be seen for the trees. The obvious is unavailable to us because we're mired in the details. What we can see so clearly in other businesses, we can't see in our own business.

I experience this in my own business. Therefore, I occasionally have someone do for me what I regularly do for other companies. As my consultant lists the opportunities I seem to be missing and the systems I need to put in place, I nod my head in agreement. I know the consultant is right, but I'm unable to bring these ideas to the foreground without help.

Awareness Changes Perception

When you buy a widget, you suddenly become aware of widgets just like yours all around. What happened was that something previously in the back of your mind suddenly was in the foreground!

How does all this apply to marketing your financial organization? First, you need to market in such a way that you're always in the foreground of your members' minds. Second, you should seek an outsider's viewpoint to see very clearly what became fuzzy because you're too close.

Of all the issues to which we are too close for making good decisions, positioning is the most difficult for business leaders to evaluate for themselves. Unfortunately, most marketing and advertising firms aren't much help and are often hurtful in creating a strategy that makes sense. Most know something about writing or doing a mailing, but they rarely know about how to help you position yourself intelligently in a way that will attract members.

So, what can you do in addition to getting outside help?

Looking outside the industry for successful positioning stories is a powerful way to clearly understand the concept of positioning and see how to best apply it.

The Domino's Model:

Before Domino's Pizza chose a position it wanted to own, it asked the obvious question:

> **"What do customers really want that our competitors aren't giving?"**

> The answer was so obvious; it's amazing it wasn't thought of earlier. People call to order pizza for one reason — and it's usually not how good the pizza tastes. They want food delivered quickly. None of Domino's competition understood this. They were happy to deliver pizza in 60 to 90 minutes, cold as the cardboard it came on.

Domino's Pizza, at its inception, completely put the pizza industry on its ear: **"Hot, delicious pizza, delivered to your door in 30 minutes or less — or it's FREE."**

Domino's looked for its competitors' weaknesses and built a guarantee around this differentiation. It worked brilliantly!

The Nordstrom Model:

Nordstrom built its success around this concept:

"If you have any problem with a purchase, for any reason, bring it back for a return with no questions asked."

A few weeks ago I purchased something at Nordstrom that I hadn't even tried on, and I told the clerk I would return it if it didn't fit. My son aptly commented, "Yeah Mom, but you probably won't."

It was true. I have hundreds of unused things I've purchased over the years thinking I could take them back. A company like Nordstrom benefits by assuming the risk that the customer might return items. They sell more as a result.

The FedEx Model:

Of course the mail industry was turned around completely when FedEx declared its USP:

EXTRAORDINARY CREDIT UNIONS 87

> "When you absolutely have to have it there overnight."

Again, the brilliance was that FedEx looked for its competitors' weaknesses — slow service and an attitude of indifference about when packages arrive — and declared a quantifiable guarantee that let people know FedEx was different and how that difference made them better.

Do You Need a General USP for Your Credit Union, as well as Ones for All of Your Products?

Yes! Not only should you have a USP for your financial institution, but you should also have one for each product line within the credit union.

The process to develop this doesn't require a lot of time or a trip to a retreat center. In fact, I simply have many of my clients complete a USP worksheet by listing all of their competitors' weaknesses in three columns; in the fourth column they list their own strengths. Visit our Web site: www.EmmerichFinancial.com for a free copy of this USP worksheet.

After a client completes that initial exercise, I start with the question,

> "When people come to you from another financial institution, what is the number one reason they switch?"

I want to know the exact words the members use. You should ask your members. Then you can see your business from their perspective.

With that information in hand, you can begin to look for what makes you stand out from your competitors. Where do your strengths coincide with your competitors' weaknesses? How can you position yourself in your market so your potential members know you're the one that stands out in this area?

Following are some examples of our clients' departmental USPs:

Mortgage Department Examples:

For a mortgage department that had the most extensive and unique offerings of mortgages in its market area:

> "Offering more mortgage options than any other financial institution so you know you'll get the best value and parameters for you."

For a mortgage department that stands out from competitors who only accept applications locally and then pass them on to the "main office," leaving their members to fend for themselves for the next steps and closing:

> "We hold your hand from application to closing. You'll never have to hassle with calling an 800 number in a far-away city where nobody cares. Nor will you have to deal with a closing where things go wrong and nobody is accountable."

For a credit union that services its own loans:

> "Your loan will never be sold to a big-city servicing company that doesn't know you or doesn't answer the phone."

For a credit union with faster approvals than the competition:

> "Time-conscious mortgages: home loan approvals within two hours so you don't lose your chance to buy your dream house."

And of course, again, Bank of America's mortgage positioning:

> "We've eliminated 80% of up-front paperwork."

Example:

Mitch Massey of Heritage Oaks has a voice-mail message that says,

> "If I don't call you back within 27 hours, it's breakfast, lunch or dinner on me!"

I know of a financial services institution that has this guarantee:

> "Through our drive-through in five minutes or we'll give you $50."

While most credit unions are shocked by the ridiculousness of this offer, thinking someone is surely going to take advantage of it, that financial institution is laughing all the way to its own vault.

Once We Have Our Unique Selling Proposition, How Do We Promote It?

Your USP should stand out in every area of your communication and be a part of every marketing process, as well as every sales activity within your credit union.

The fastest and easiest place to immediately apply your positioning is in drafting sales questions for each staff member that correspond to his or her departmental positioning statement.

Let's use each of the previous positioning examples and build some questions around them. The mortgage department with the most extensive and unique offerings in its market area may want to ask its members:

> "How important is it for you to do business with a financial institution that has the most mortgage options, giving you the comfort of knowing you will get the best mortgage with the best specifications and the best value?"

The mortgage department that stands out from its competitors by taking the loan application and staying with it all the way to conclusion may ask:

> "How important is it to have someone working with you from application to closing who insures that your mortgage goes easily and quickly, as opposed to most financial institutions, where, after they take your application, it goes into a far-off land to be processed and you're on your own if you have a problem?"

For the credit union, that services its own mortgages:

> "How important is it to you to have someone with whom you can talk locally if you have questions or concerns now or in the future about your mortgage? With most mortgages that are sold in the secondary market, you are given an 800 number —thus making it nearly impossible to find a human being to answer a question for you."

For the time-conscious credit union that can assure fast approval:

> "How important is it for you to work with a credit union that will approve your loan within two hours, so you save time and make sure you don't miss an opportunity to buy your dream house?"

Finally, if I had worked for Bank of America after their 2002 Winter Olympics advertising blitz, my lead question would have been:

> "How important is it for you to eliminate 80 percent of all up-front paperwork to make your life simpler and easier?"

Use Your USP EVERYWHERE

In addition to building your positioning into each of your departments' sales-profiling questions, it is important to build it into your referral systems, marketing letters, advertisements and public relations campaigns.

The BOUNCE BACK — A Sound of Success!

An excellent positioning statement bounces back to you — you hear your words bounce back through other people. When your members start to say to you what you've said to them, that's great. When they start telling potential members who come into your credit union and those potential members use your words as well, you then know you've arrived at a solid and powerful positioning statement and have done a good job of getting it out to the market.

When you have members who are referring you, you want to make sure that they so clearly understand your differentiation that they can say your positioning statement as easily and as powerfully as you can.

Summary

Very few financial institutions have learned the basics of how to position themselves. Even fewer have started to create a positioning statement. This creates tremendous opportunity for those who take this task seriously. Begin now to find the biggest unmet need being expressed by your competition's members. Then move quickly to build your systems to meet that need and the marketing to own that position before someone else claims it as their territory.

Only by clearly positioning your important differentiation can you price yourself more profitably and create a steady stream of referral prospects. Once clear on your differentiation, build your marketing, your materials, your systems, and everything else around that positioning. FedEx created the plan to make sure their packages actually got there overnight. So, too, must you do something out of the ordinary to put you in a different league than your competitors and have them sorely wishing they would have thought of it first.

> **The more you build on your positioning to make it solid and obvious, the more likely your members will believe you are truly the owner of that positioning.**

Unique Selling Proposition Worksheet

Credit Union Name _____

Competitor 1 Weaknesses	Competitor 2 Weaknesses	Competitor 3 Weaknesses	Our Strengths (detailed)	Member Needs and Wants

Action Plan for Implementing Strategies in Chapter 3				
Action to Take	Responsible Person	Results	Start Date	Target Date
Benefits				

4 Breakthrough Strategies to Maximize Results

Change Your Strategy:

Create a New Strategy for a More Competitive Financial Institution Environment

Probably the responsibility most overlooked by credit union executives is to create a solid strategy.

With brokerage analysts projecting a challenging decade ahead, ignoring a shift to a new strategy could be devastating. Business as usual will almost guarantee results falling substantially below the norm.

But if consumer financial services get tough, does it have to get tough for you too?

Southwest Airlines was recently ranked as the top return-on-investment stock over the last 30 years. In an industry that is known for bailouts, bankruptcies and difficult earnings, Southwest's successful strategy has been impervious to current market conditions.

> **The fastest and easiest way to transform your financial institution is to change your strategy.**

Reviews of hundreds of plans have led me to at least one certain conclusion: Most credit unions are tactical, not strategic. They're more worried about daily transactions than they are committed to creating a solid and powerful guiding plan. They list goals and tactics, but they have no big-picture strategy.

What's missing for many credit unions is a focus on engineering a business implementation approach that maximizes revenue, retains members, penetrates each account, and positions the credit union clearly in its market as superior in some area that creates sustainable and exciting results.

What Is and Isn't a Strategy?

Chances are, what you're thinking is wrong.

> **Strategy is the explanation of your entire operating approach and why and how every element of it integrates, advances, deploys, and manifests the highest vision and outcome you desire.**

Example of a Meaningful Strategy:

We will attract a lot of members with a break-even product and then, due to our profiling strategy, we will immediately cross-sell them a minimum of three additional products within the first month. Our average client retention will be 15 years due to our system of contacting and counseling them at least yearly — and more often for identified high-potential members.

That's a good strategy. Then, your tactics of advertising, marketing, and selling are in alignment with your strategy.

It appears that the strategy for Commerce Bank (as referred to earlier) is to go after the neglected retail clients with a "no-to-low" fee approach and hours that accommodate the working schedule, keep overhead low, have brand consistencies, and create a position of being "America's Most Convenient Bank."

How Do You Create the Ultimate Strategy?

1. List the highest performing companies, both within and outside the credit union industry, that have created sustainable results. Look to companies like Walgreen's, Nordstrom, Domino's Pizza, and other retailers who have excelled in certain areas.

2. For each company, list the strategies it employs. Ask, "How are they accomplishing this?"

3. You should list at least 50 strategies. Then you can evaluate those from which you want to borrow or combine two or more to create your ultimate strategy.

4. Don't forget to work backward by understanding what you really want to have happen. Do you want to be progressive in the area of technology? Do you want to be high-touch and have a large staff to accommodate that strategy, or do you want to be a high-volume credit union with high efficiency but less service?

Changing your strategy, if properly deployed, managed, and systematized, can double, triple, or quadruple your growth rate. It revitalizes your people by enrolling them in a bigger picture of greatness. It breathes life into what is often a tired approach and exponentially increases the return from your resources.

Questions You Need to Ask Yourself to Create Your Strategy

Your strategy is only as good as the quality of your questions. If I asked you what your strengths are, you would probably say things like, "I'm smart. I'm a hard worker. I get people around me fired up." You'd probably add a few other surface-level answers.

What if, on the other hand, I asked you much deeper-level questions like these?

- What were you good at as a kid?
- What awards did you win in high school?
- What did your mother or father tell you was outstanding about you as a child?
- What is it you do better than anyone else?
- What's the one thing you do that gives you the most energy?
- What elements about that get you excited?

You can imagine that the answers would suddenly become much stronger, well thought out, unique, and meaningful. The same thing happens with the questions you ask when creating your strategy.

When you ask your group the typical strategic-planning questions, you'll probably receive only trite, expected answers that are far more the "persona" of your credit union than the real potential and power of your credit union. Typical strategic-planning questions include:

- What are your strengths?
- What are your weaknesses?
- What are your opportunities?
- What are your threats?

Instead, try asking questions like:

- When members come to us from other financial institutions, why do they choose us?
- Who are our present members?
- What is their profile?
- How are they similar and how are they dissimilar?
- How do we segment them?
- What would be the profile of our ideal new members?
- How is their profile different from that of our existing members?
- What members have we lost and why?
- How is their profile different from that of our satisfied members?

With questions of this nature, you get real and meaningful information about where opportunities and strengths intersect, which can lead you to create a powerful strategy.

It's not uncommon for credit unions to think their strategy session is simply a listing of projected goals for loan quality, growth, ROA, and capital. Without asking the right questions and building a strategy around the answers, the probability of reaching those goals is low.

A complete list of thought-provoking, strategy-building questions is presented on our Web site, www.EmmerichFinancial.com. These questions will help you develop the kinds of conversations that will create a sound and powerful direction for your organization.

Creating a strategy and a vision are two of the most important jobs of leadership. Doing these well is rare. Those who do these tasks well AND understand the psychology of getting their people to buy in and implement their plan will be far more able to compete in today's tough markets.

The following abbreviated list is for your immediate reference. Refer to the complete list in each heading on our Web site.

Strategic Planning Questions to Prompt a Successful Mindset

Complete listing: www.EmmerichFinancial.com

Vision

1. What is the key message or phrase that describes our organization?
2. What is our personal vision of how the organization would look or provide services in the future?

Ideal Conditions

(A view of the future state of the organization when the vision is reached.)

1. What will the culture of our organization be like?
2. What kind of relationships will we have with
    - Members?
    - Employees?
    - Community?
3. If we lived our values in an extraordinary way, what would happen?

Mission

1. Why does our organization exist? Why are we needed?
2. What business are we in?

EXTRAORDINARY CREDIT UNIONS

3. What makes our business unique?

Members' Needs and Wants

1. Who are our present members?
2. What is their profile?
   - How are they similar and how are they dissimilar?
   - How do we segment them?
3. What are our members' articulated needs? Unarticulated needs?
4. How do we influence member loyalty?

Employees' Needs and Wants

1. What are the articulated needs of our employees?
2. What are the unarticulated needs of our employees?
3. Do we have mutual trust and respect:
   - Between employees?
   - Between employees and management?
   - Between employees and members?
   - Between employees and suppliers?

Competition

1. Who are our competitors today and what are their strengths and weaknesses?
2. In what areas that members care about are we stronger than our competitors?

Marketplace

1. Fundamentally, what business are we in?
2. What business should we be in?

3. What is our market niche?
4. Where is the market going?
5. What is the biggest unmet need of our competitors' customer?

Technology

1. Do we have the proper technology to be successful reaching our vision?
2. If not, can we develop or purchase it?
3. What technologies are emerging? How might they influence us?

Internal Conditions

1. Are we capable of reaching our vision?
2. If not, what are we lacking and what must be done to reach it?
3. What are our core competencies? What do we do better than anyone else?
4. What core competencies do we need to acquire to succeed in the future?

External Conditions

1. What economic trends are likely to have the most impact on our business over the next three to five years?
2. How will environmental enlightenment affect us?
3. What effects could the national or local economy have on our business?

Strengths

1. What do we do best?

EXTRAORDINARY CREDIT UNIONS

    2. Do our members really care about this strength?
    3. What are some untapped resources?

Weaknesses

1. What are our most critical vulnerabilities in the eyes of our members?
2. What are our most critical vulnerabilities in the eyes of our employees?
3. What are our most critical vulnerabilities in the eyes of our competitors?

Opportunities

1. What are the unmet needs of our potential members?
2. In what ways are we technically superior to our competitors?
3. What market niches best fit our specialties?

Threats

1. In what market and product areas are we in the declining phase?
2. What negative impact could the economy have on our organization?
3. What are our limitations? Why?

Financial

1. What are the expectations for our revenue growth percentage over the next five years?
2. Do we have sufficient capital to carry out our plans?

Requirements

1. What are the four most essential requirements for successful performance for any organization in our business?
2. In addition to our current services, are there any additional areas into which we should consider expanding?

Products/Services

1. What are examples of clearly successful and unsuccessful products and services?
2. How does the pricing of our product/service compare to our competition?
3. How can we better package our products for our identified niches?

Structure

1. Is our organization structured in the best possible way?
2. Do we have the right people in place to carry out our plans?
3. Do we have successful efforts underway to improve and innovate these key processes?
4. Do we have a sales management system that works?

To thoroughly explore every category given above, review the complete list of 160 questions on our Web site: www.EmmerichFinancial.com.

Summary

Only by digging deeply for the answers to these questions can you build a strategy based on a sound premise. Many a brilliantly laid-out strategy was built on faulty premises, which later led to the demise of the company. Kmart, which started the same year as Wal-Mart and Target, created a strategy of trying to have the appeal of Target and the pricing of Wal-Mart — neither was possible. They had no idea who they were, and the "follow-the-leader" strategy ranks right up there with other criminal mismanagement.

Many credit unions have a "follow-the-leader" strategy that doesn't speak to a uniqueness that is of benefit to their market nor employs a delivery mechanism that allows differentiation. A saying my father often repeated to my siblings and me throughout the high-school years would be profound advice to many a credit union who listened: "If they all jumped off the cliff, would you?"

The perfect "jumping-off-the-cliff" example was the rush for banks to open branches in grocery stores. It wasn't until a substantial amount had been invested in what would be a horrible public relations move to unravel, that banks finally spent the time to analyze the situation and discovered that most grocery store branches were NOT profitable.

Only by encouraging a deeper level of truth can you get to the core of the issues that need to be answered. Leadership must foster a safe place to "tell the truth" at a deeper level. Temper tantrums when ideas are challenged will only result in a reduction of sharing by your team in the future.

Most credit union CEOs spend less time working on their strategy than they do making sure the building maintenance is handled. Create the venue and the event that will allow all of your staff to align in the same direction — one that creates the best possible future for your financial institution.

Action Plan for Implementing Strategies in Chapter 4

Action to Take	Responsible Person	Results	Start Date	Target Date

Benefits

5 Breakthrough to Highly Effective Marketing

"Business has only two basic functions — marketing and innovation." Peter Drucker

Marketing is the consistent and systematic approach to get your current members to use you more, stay longer, and elevate the quality of your members and referrals.

You will discover in this chapter how you can easily and quickly do both. As you read, I encourage you to ask yourself the following key questions:

1. Which of the ideas presented here should be the basis of my marketing and the areas to focus on first?

   _____
   _____
   _____
   _____

2. How can I use these strategies to maximize the growth of my credit union?

   _____
   _____
   _____
   _____

3. How can I improve my ability to build relationships within my marketplace even before the initial sale takes place?

_____
_____
_____
_____

4. How can I add value to my relationships with my existing members?

_____
_____
_____
_____

5. Which of these strategies and tactics will have the best impact in my market?

_____
_____
_____
_____

The Out-of-Touch Marketing Trap of Disbelief

Before we start, it's important to acknowledge that most marketing is based on out-of-touch philosophies and is delivered in such a way that fed-up consumers do not believe it anyway.

We can create a marketing strategy that works only by understanding the fact that over 70 percent of U.S. adults believe marketers exploit and mislead them. When you use this fact as a basis for your marketing strategies, you will then be able to reach your market in such a way that they will believe and accept your marketing.

Yet we still see credit unions going against these odds and throwing marketing money down the hole. They use advertising that depends on clichés and rhetoric, which does more to turn off potential members than to engage them to use the credit union.

Example:

A recent financial services institution advertisement promoted:

"5-Point Member Service!"

What exactly does this mean? Where is the value to the member? Interestingly, this particular institution was known for having below-average member service in its market area.

This institution broke the two most important rules of advertising:

Rule #1: *Don't say you are what you aren't — because when people discover you're not, you'll look even worse.*

Rule #2: *If there isn't at least an implied promise, don't waste your money!*

Since we already know intuitively that marketing campaigns based on weak, erroneous statements and hackneyed expressions tend to be ineffective, and since research shows that people just don't believe them, one question is obvious:

What works?

All marketing strategies must be built on the three motivators that will prompt people to use services:

1. People they know or know about.
2. People they trust.
3. People to whom they relate and that they feel relate to them.

I am so grateful for an insight a boss gave me over 20 years ago. He used to incessantly repeat this principle of success that he wanted his employees to understand and embroider on their underwear:

> **"People don't do business with organizations— people do business with people."**

With this in mind, know that all strategies and tactics in this book are based on "relationship" marketing, as opposed to "throw-it-against-the-wall-and-see-if-it-sticks" type marketing. Relationship marketing is the exact opposite of what is recommended by most marketing firms. Because they are paid a percentage of the advertising dollars you pay out to media, they tend to promote radio, television, and newsprint advertising. However, the fact is those mediums often give you the least effective results.

When I was hired to start a new financial institution, I suddenly had to do its marketing function — something I was not prepared for. I can share with you now that I knew nothing about marketing. I had never taken a marketing course in my life; I had never even read a marketing book. I started my career as a commercial lender and, suffice it to say, was not exposed to ANY great marketing minds.

So I did what almost every marketer does: I followed last year's budget. Sure, I sponsored the 4-H calf at the fair and placed a few highly ineffective ads. They either looked like those we had done in the past or were placed through ad reps from the local paper who didn't have any better understanding of effective marketing than I did. Actually, since the newspaper ad reps I knew did not have the finance experience I had, they probably understood far less about why people buy from one financial institution as opposed to another or what motivates people to change their financial services relationships.

Since that time, I have studied with some of the greatest marketing minds of our time, and now I realize how much I was missing the mark back in those early days. Interestingly, though, while I was missing the mark, the organization where I managed the marketing department still grew infinitely faster and more profitably than our competitors. This tells me how much worse my competitors were at understanding marketing strategy.

Effective and Ineffective Marketing Strategies

Over the years, my consulting experience with thousands of financial institutions has provided me with the opportunity to witness the marketing strategies they use and the results they receive. It is obvious that the results differ greatly between those who follow smart marketing approaches and those who do not.

Smart Marketing Strategies

Marketing strategies that work are based on the following:

1. Understanding what your market wants;
2. Recognizing the truth; and
3. Listening and learning.

Too Close to the Problem to See It?

> While flying across the country a few years ago, I had the opportunity to sit in front of two women who were on their way to Las Vegas for a gambling trip. My mother would have called them "bar women." With their prematurely wrinkled skin and their hair dried out from too many bad perms, they reapplied their eye shadow, the color of rotten fruit, at least three times during that three-hour flight.
>
> Try as we might, the people in my row wanted desperately not to hear any more of their conversation. But, because they apparently never learned about "indoor voices," there was no escaping their loud and raspy talk.
>
> "You've been married ten times?" one said to the other.
>
> "What was wrong with all of them?"
>
> Yes, it's clear to you and me that it probably wasn't "THEM" that was the problem. The woman, like many of us, was too close to the problem to see clearly what the problem was.

The same happens in credit unions. We are so close to our market that we think we understand what it wants, and then we are surprised to find that we've missed the mark entirely.

Caution: Marketing Studies Are Not a Cure-all!

As strongly as I want to impress that you understand your market, it is more important to note the following:

> **Of all the marketing expenditures invested in low-return approaches, the biggest culprit is the "marketing study."**

To borrow a line from Jerry Seinfeld, "It's not that there is anything wrong" with marketing studies, it's that they don't always tell the whole picture.

The Problem

I've seen financial services institutions spend $50,000 to $250,000 or more on a marketing study and at the same time deliberately ignore business that comes their way. To more than 90 percent of callers inquiring about rates, they give ONLY the rates and nothing more! They let potential members, who have taken the time to call, hang up the phone without an attempt to earn their business.

The Solution

What would be the point of knowing more about who your members could be if you have not developed the systems and attitudes to convert people who are calling you? Those who call you are already waving their arms and asking you to let them know how you can serve them and how they can do business with you. They are begging to have you invite them in, not to be indifferent to their financial service needs.

You must understand the market. But first, you need to invest in the highest return, lowest-hanging-fruit areas.

Basic Marketing Principle

If you don't know how to reach your members, or worse yet, if you don't know how to turn potential members into members, it makes little sense to do a market research study.

Where to Get Market Research?

1. **Use National Research Studies:** Often, national research can give you most of the information you need.

2. **Go to Your Members and Potential Members:** Most of your market research can be done with little expense by talking to your members and potential members and finding how they differ from national trends.

3. **Identify the Ten Most Influential People:** Making contacts with influential people in new markets allows you to find out what they think is missing and what they would want from you.

> **Another Basic Marketing Principle**
>
> Invest your first marketing dollars in
> immediate-return strategies.

What Are Those Immediate-Return Strategies?

Strategy 1: Spend the majority of your marketing dollars on marketing to your current members.

There are three ways to spend your marketing dollars:

1. To attract potential new members;
2. To engage current members to use you more and more often; and
3. To train your employees at all levels to be evangelists.

What's Best?

Of the three, the strategy with the highest return on investment is to market to your current members. However, this is true only if your employees have reasonable skill and plan to cross-sell and convert inquiries into booked business. If your employees do not, then the first marketing dollars should be invested in your people to perfect their skills in converting inquirers into users of multiple services.

What's Least Productive and Stifles Growth?

The lowest return on your money will be from marketing to find new members. Ironically, this happens to be the highest expenditure of most marketing programs.

Why? We are brainwashed. It is a result of an unconscious and reactive marketing approach called "letting the tail wag the dog."

> This creates marketing that is driven by media salespeople who receive commissions based on the money spent with them.

The media marketers win, but you, your potential members, and your members do not! Reverse that situation and spend your marketing dollars to produce results.

Smart credit union marketers focus on the best possible return on investment. They know that current members are statistically proven to offer this return. Therefore, they focus the majority of their marketing dollars on penetration and retention of their current members.

How? Here are four of the most successful ways that many top-performing credit unions said they get their current members to bond with them:

1. Sponsoring meetings for their members to learn new things from guest lecturers
2. Sending out personalized mailings
3. Making consistently scheduled calls to coach members toward their financial goals

Strategy 2: Create a Buzz.

The first time someone tells me I should see a certain movie, I don't think much of it. When the second person tells me, "That movie's great! You ought to see it," I feel compelled to read up on it. And by the third time, I literally stop what I'm doing and go see the movie. Why? It has created a buzz. When people are buzzing about it, people hear about it. The result: I feel like everyone has seen the movie except me, and the urge to be in equilibrium with my fellow man is too overwhelming to ignore.

The same is true for credit union marketing.

In his insightful book, *The Tipping Point: How Little Things Can Make a Big Difference*, Malcolm Gladwell defines this buzz phenomenon as "The Tipping Point — that magic moment when an idea, trend, or social behavior crosses a threshold, tips, and spreads like wildfire."

Example:

> Let's take a new style of Nikes. Without the right buzz, they'll most likely be overlooked by consumers (as are most new products). However, if they're prominently worn by a successful Olympian, you can bet that they'll fly off the shelves in no time.

Example:

> Here's another example of a buzz-generated feeding frenzy. Looking for a high-impact yet low-cost way of creating a buzz about a new branch? One of our clients did the following:

One month before opening their new location, they ran a series of newspaper ads. Each mentioned the branch's grand opening, featured member testimonials, and the ads grew in size as the month wore on.

To complement these ads, they also did a face-to-face publicity blitz. Over a two-day period, they sent their employees out into the community to visit as many local businesses as they could. They then gave each decision maker and the person who escorted them to the decision maker a homemade oversized cookie that was decoratively wrapped with cellophane, ribbon, and an attached business card.

The cookies turned out to be great icebreakers and helped facilitate over 205 get-to-know-us visits! In fact, many of those decision makers expressed genuine interest in doing business with the new branch — and that's not all. The institution is still following up on their very hot list of leads.

The infamous "cookie visits" and growing newspaper ads also got the whole town talking about this new and innovative financial institution. While most credit unions just put up a sign, open their doors and blindly wait for a rush of members, (which, of course, rarely happens), this institution created a low-cost, and highly effective buzz strategy. It not only got them immediate business, but it also positioned them as a mover and a shaker in town. Now, the "tired old traditional financial institutions" in that town had to struggle to hang on to their business.

EXTRAORDINARY CREDIT UNIONS

Have a CECU magazine w/ advertising (pictures of cars from car dealers

What's the long and the short of it?

> **If you want a fast and easy way to market your credit union, create a buzz.**

System to Implement:

Do a unique publicity blitz to create a "buzz" about your credit union's innovative services.

You may ask, "How do you get a great idea for a unique publicity blitz?"

There are many ways. Here are two of the greatest:

1. The quickest, easiest, and most practical way is to hold a brainstorming session with your employees. Also invite a marketing consultant (preferably someone who knows something about the credit union industry, as well as marketing) and brainstorm. Don't let the marketing consultant dominate in the idea-giving area, but allow that person to bait and spearhead the group. You will be amazed how creative your employees can be when given guidance and inspiration and when they're allowed to express their thoughts freely.

   By the way, a side effect of your employees feeling "in on things" is their ongoing spirit of cooperation and motivation. This continues throughout their regular workweek and promotes more and better business.

2. Another way to generate outstanding buzz promotion ideas is to form a mastermind group with people from a variety of industries. Have them brainstorm some wonderful ideas. They will be remarkable.

Two friends of mine did just this when they wanted to create a buzz about their forthcoming book, *The One-Minute Millionaire*. At that time they already held the number one position in their fields. Who is more known as a motivator than Mark Victor Hansen of *Chicken Soup for the Soul* fame with his 75 *New York Times* bestsellers? And who better to advise you on becoming a millionaire than the number one millionaire-maker in the world, Robert G. Allen, with his signature book, *Nothing Down,* which happened to be *the* number-one-selling financial book of the 1980s, as well as the author of other *New York Times* bestsellers?

One would not think these authors needed help coming up with creative marketing ideas, but they both believe in the mastermind principle for creating a buzz. So they asked 40 of their top marketing friends from all walks of business to come together for a day and mastermind how to pre-sell one million copies of their new book.

They created their buzz by having 100 people in 100 cities each holding 100 copies of the books in their hands. That's 1 million books pre-publication! But their ultimate goal is to create one million enlightened millionaires in the next decade. (An enlightened millionaire is one who gives back to make the world a better place for all to enjoy now and in the future.) Such creative thinking came out of that one mastermind session they held in one day — they generated ideas far beyond what just the two of them would have come up with.

Think of what you, too, can do when you mastermind with an outstanding group of people assembled in one room or via a conference call for an hour or two once a week, once a month, or once a year!

There is no limit to creative thinking.

Strategy 3: Clearly Define a Niche Market.

Most community charter credit unions employ a generic approach to marketing and rarely go after a targeted group. While this may have worked in the past, it certainly doesn't work today; there is, quite simply, too much competition.

Did you know that, in today's crowded marketplace, the credit unions that clearly identify a niche market and go after it tend to have higher growth rates and better member retention?

And, remarkably, those potential members not in the niche market tend to be more attracted for some odd reason, and business tends to grow!

Example:

A great example of niche marketing's power is the Marlboro dynasty. Jay Conrad Levinson, the author of *Guerrilla Marketing*, was hired to help Marlboro grow its market share from one of the lowest in the industry. His suggestion? Find a niche.

After extensive research, they decided to focus on men. They then created a macho, rugged image/lifestyle that they felt their target market would idolize. The result? You guessed it: the Marlboro man — a true man's man, complete with a chiseled jaw and bow-legged stance who commanded his world by smoking a Marlboro.

This niche campaign made Marlboro the number one cigarette of choice among men in just a few years. And, remarkably, it made Marlboro the most preferred cigarette for women too! Conventional wisdom would tell us women would run away from Marlboro. This is definitely a lesson from which we all can learn much.

Actually, this "niche phenomenon" has worked for several of the top-performing financial institutions we've interviewed. Many who promoted themselves as commercial institutions attracted more commercial business at higher profit margins AND seemed to be a magnet for retail business — oftentimes as much as financial services institutions who did not brand themselves. However, these "specialty" institutions were able to command premium rates from their commercial members since they were perceived as being "specialists."

Many credit unions brand by the markets they go after: baby boomers, Gen-Xer's, women, small business, to name a few. Others brand by the way they do business: speed of delivery, professional consultative coaching, knowing all their members' names, and more.

Choose the Right Niche by Asking the Right Questions

You'll quickly learn that the success of your niche marketing is in **choosing the right niche**. A few questions you should ask prior to branding your credit union include the following:

- Is this market growing or declining?
- Are the sales and/or incomes of this market growing or declining?
- What spin-off opportunities does this market offer?
- Can you uniquely position yourself in this market? How so?
- Does this market really need what you're offering?
- Can you repackage your products to better fit the needs of this market?

Regarding accessibility to these markets, ask yourself:

- Does this market have an established networking chain?
- Are there clubs or associations that will help you penetrate this market and create a buzz?
- Are there newsletters, trade magazines, or any targeted communication tools that will make it easier for you to reach this market?
- Does this market have available lead sources or generators?
- Is there a common culture — recreationally, ethnically, or business wise — on which you can capitalize?

Abe Lincoln once said,

> "If I had six days to chop down a tree, I would spend five days sharpening my axe!"

That being said, niche marketing is only as successful as the research it's based on. So do your homework and choose your niche markets wisely. You're sure to find success as long as you identify a group that is growing and successful, fits in well with what you do, is one that you like working with, and, most importantly, networks with others so they create a buzz and refer their friends and colleagues!

Strategy 4: Create a Formal Referral Program for Centers of Influence.

Question: What is the little known secret of high-performing credit unions with rapid growth and low member acquisition costs?

Answer: A formalized referral program!
Accountants, lawyers, realtors, hospitals, and large businesses alike can send a continual stream of prospects to your door. Obviously their clients trust them. If these prime businesses think your credit union is the best around, their customers will too.

Question: Need more convincing on why you should target referrals?

Answer: Research proves that referrals:
- cost the least to acquire;
- buy more;
- stay longer;
- negotiate less;
- appreciate you more; and
- refer their friends more often.

Easy Four-Step Getting-Started Referral Plan

Step #1: Identify Your Ideal Referral/Member.

Identify your demographics for each of the following categories:
- ✓ Income
- ✓ Age
- ✓ Gender
- ✓ Neighborhood
- ✓ Net worth
- ✓ Type of business
- ✓ Educational background
- ✓ Marital status
- ✓ Position
- ✓ Hobbies
- ✓ Association memberships
- ✓ Religious affiliation
- ✓ Other demographics that are important to you

Note: Your demographics will vary depending on the product area you're promoting.

It is critical to identify the demographics for each one of the products/services you are offering. Of course, after you identify each product's most compatible users, you can then better tailor your referral marketing efforts toward them.

Step #2: Identify Sources That Already Cater to Your Potential Members.

Make a list for each of the following referral sources, and then prioritize them based on their leveraging potential:
- ✓ Current members
- ✓ Employees
- ✓ Competitors
- ✓ Association members
- ✓ Relatives of members, prospects, employees, etc.
- ✓ Accountants
- ✓ Attorneys
- ✓ Realtors
- ✓ Relocation specialists in the HR departments of large local firms
- ✓ Others

Step #3: Build Your Case for Referrals.

The most important part of creating a successful referral program is positively distinguishing yourself from your competition — preferably in a way that matters to your ideal market.

Example — Ineffective Approach:

> Most mortgage lenders ask realtors for referrals in this way: "Hey, we'd sure like to have you bring your people to us." This rarely works because it delivers no benefit

to the realtors and it doesn't distinguish your business in any way.

Example — Effective Approach:

Mortgage lenders will see better results if they say the following:

"I know the most important thing in a realtor's world is to get more deals done fast and effortlessly so your customers will do repeat business with you and refer their friends to you. And we have an easier way to make this happen!

"Any client you refer to us will receive a weekly report listing what we've received, what's still outstanding (BENEFIT), and how to get it (DIFFERENCE). We'll also guarantee that you'll NEVER have a last-minute disaster at closing. This is one of the best times to position yourself for referrals and future business.

"If you refer your clients to us, we'll also make absolutely sure that their hands are held throughout the entire loan process, making them feel smart and competent. And, in the process, we'll make you look even better, thereby reinforcing their decision in choosing you now — and in the future."

Step #4: Offer Something of Value for FREE or at a Discount.

Your offer to a realtor could be: "And, let your customers know that because of our relationship, if they mention you sent them, they'll save $150 off the cost of the appraisal."

For the most success, make sure that your giveaway is at a low cost to you but with a high-perceived value to potential referrals. (Again, good research will really pay off!)

Also, make sure to train your staff to ensure that referral members bring ALL of their business when their account is set up. The last thing you need is for a referral to be greeted by an "order-taker" who doesn't penetrate the value of the account.

Of course, you should always make your referral sources look great in their clients' eyes; this will ensure they keep sending you more!

How to Create an Effective Referral System in Your Credit Union

Sit down with your management team now and create FIVE different referral systems you can implement immediately for different centers of influence and/or for different product lines.

Once you have them in place, always remember to thank your referral sources often and lavish them with praise, meaningful gifts, and correspondence.

Strategy 5: Schedule a Philosophical Lobotomy.

EXTRAORDINARY CREDIT UNIONS

A credit union in Texas looking to grow its business recently contacted me. Its executive started by asking me a few questions, which I promptly answered. I then asked him a list of questions that I felt needed consideration. He finally remarked, "Hey, this is interesting. I called to interview you, but you're asking me all the questions!"

Actually, in my dealings, I have found this is a very common experience. It's only by asking detailed questions that I can determine if I'll be a good fit with my potential clients. Through a two-way question-and-answer session, I can quickly unveil what type of leader a credit union has.

My experience has taught me that there are two kinds of leaders:
1) the kind who, if led to water, will create a distribution center ensuring years of hydration for herself, her members, and her employees; and
2) the kind who, if led to water, will fill only her own canteen, then walk away ensuring eventual dehydration for herself and everyone else.

After interviewing CEOs of numerous top-performing credit unions, I found their secret to success to be much the same: an undying commitment to their team and members. They understood that if they always kept the interests of their employees and members in mind, the numbers would take care of themselves — and usually this would cause a dramatic increase in growth as well! It's the principle of "authentic marketing."

Example:

When Adrienne, an intern who transcribed my interviews with top-performing CEOs, finished her project, she said,

"I just love these people. Their sincerity is amazing. I literally want to call them up and ask to be their friend!"

Coincidence? I think not.

A Tip from Those at the Top

Top-performing leaders never allow "ice-in-the-veins" business transactions to occur. They are successful, and make many friends, because they sincerely care about their people and their members.

Example:

The movie, *A Beautiful Mind,* portrays how Nobel Prize winner John Nash spent decades committed to overcoming his battle with schizophrenia. It was this commitment that enabled him to be open to help from others, including his wife, who said, "The problem is not up here, John (pointing to his head); the problem is down here (pointing to his heart)."

Example:

Robert Johnson, the famous Jungian psychologist known for his work on transforming the psyche, notes that most men and many women suffer from what he terms "the wounded feeling function." In this state, people never truly appreciate and enjoy life. His studies have also found that the majority of men don't address this "wounded feeling function" until they're 50. Up until this time they try to heal their wounds by setting higher goals, getting a nicer car/fancier house, or even by trading-in "the old wife." Between the ages of 45 and 50, the need to dull the pain takes on a frenzied level of energy.

However, they come to realize that these quick fixes do not dull their pain. The pain is within and can only be solved internally. It isn't until about age 50 that they find the path to joy is by helping others. They are driven to a purpose outside themselves as the path to their own healing.

To sum it up, if you want to thrive as a person and as an organization, the key is to focus on making a meaningful and powerful difference in the lives of those around you. Build your systems, products, services, and employee practices to help your members thrive, and then you, too, will win. After all, the more you help others get what they want, the more you'll receive as well.

A Tip from the Top

The Power Comes from Focusing—Out!

Strategy 6: Recognize the Value of Direct Mail.

In the world of radio, TV, newsprint, and other advertising outreaches, direct mail (as long as it is done right) is your best shot at an excellent return on your investment. I know, you hear the words "direct mail" and you think "junk mail." But direct mail only becomes "junk mail" when it is done wrong. Doing it wrong includes sending it to people who aren't interested in what you're offering or sending glossy color stuffers that are so generic nobody looks at them.

If you take the time to accurately target your direct mail, it can be the most powerful, effective, and low-cost advertising available.

Imagine the cost of hiring a lender or business development officer to call on thousands of potential members. Costly? You bet!

What if instead you leverage this professional's message through a brilliantly enticing sales letter? It would reach the same number of potential members at a faster rate with less expense.

Sounds too good to be true, doesn't it?

If this is really true, which it is, then why don't more financial institutions use direct mail? Simple. Because there are no "direct mail" sales reps running around door-to-door selling credit unions on using direct mail like TV, radio, and newspaper sales reps do. Broadcast and print media always offer an enticing advertising "special of the month" that their reps sell and sell and sell. Direct mail does not ask you to use it. The media's in-your-face advertising sales approach prompts businesses to buy their advertising, often without real regard to or a solid comparative analysis of the return on investment.

Here's your wakeup call:

> **Create an Effective Direct Mail Sales Campaign and Grow!**

Use the following three main components to create your own cost-effective, wildly successful direct mail program . . .

- Create a targeted mailing list.
- Use a highly compelling offer.
- Employ top-notch copy writing.

Compile a Great List.

For direct mail, there are essentially three kinds of lists:
- Compiled lists;
- Direct response lists; and
- Current member lists.

Compiled lists draw names from directories, such as phone books and governmental records.

Direct response lists include potential members who had to do something to be added to the list, such as purchase a certain type of product. Obviously, this type of list is much more effective than a compiled list, because the contacts are somewhat qualified.

Your current member list, however, is the most effective by far.

Many top-performing credit unions I've worked with have in common a somewhat unique, new, and highly successful business strategy. Instead of continually searching for new members, they focus on member retention and penetration.

A Tip from Top-performing Credit Unions

Focus on existing members!

Even with limited marketing resources, these top-performing credit unions have discovered that by spending ALL of their time, funds, and energy on their current members, they get the most profitable return on investment. It would seem to make sense to follow those who are accomplishing what you want to accomplish. In this case, make sure to keep your current members in mind when devising your next direct mail campaign; this could be just the key you need to unlock a wealth of new opportunities.

Your Survey

Once you've identified the group to target your marketing, you'll need to create a survey. It should be designed to identify your most powerful and enticing offer. It's not so much <u>what do your members want</u> but <u>what factors cause people to buy that you want to know about.</u> Thus, your survey should focus on questions that ascertain your group's psychological motivations and behaviors.

Sample Questions

- What did you like most (i.e., a product or service) about your previous financial institution?
- What did you like least?
- How could your previous financial institution have improved its products or services?
- Why did you choose your current financial institution?
- What additional services or products would you like your financial institution to offer?
- What frustrates you the most about financial services in general?

Sample Demographics

For consumers:
- Age
- Income
- Marital status
- Magazine subscriptions
- Current neighborhood
- Number of family members
- Employment type

Conducting Your Survey

Now that you've created your survey, there are four ways to execute it.

- **Telephone** — Have one or several of your staff members call your marketing list and conduct the survey over the phone.

- **Mail/Fax** — Send a cover letter to your marketing list via the mail or a fax that thanks them for their business and asks for their help in making your credit union even better. (Note: This method is the slowest but also the least costly.)

- **On-site** — Offer your members a free gift for filling out the survey before they leave the building.

- **Online** — This is quick, easy, and inexpensive — and the results are immediate. If you are not using online methods to stay in touch with your members, you should consider all possibilities.

Analyze Your Survey

After you've conducted your survey, compile and analyze the results for any commonalities. This will help your list broker find you a more targeted mailing list.

Example:

> Instead of just saying, "We'd like a list of people who live in the area," say, "We want a list of potential members who need our services, who live within three miles of our new branch." Your survey will give you the specifics that will help you target your market more effectively.
>
> Again, it's important that you focus on your best list — your current member list — first. If you'd still like to target new members, you will also save a lot of time and money by targeting those who are similar to your existing members.

> **Once you know who they are and what they want, give it to them!**

Why Direct Mail is Your Best Return on Investment Marketing Tactic

When you understand what the market wants, know that there is not one market. There are thousands of different markets, all with different needs. Direct mail allows you to give different messages to different markets, and it increases your sales potential far better than any other marketing tool.

You're probably thinking this is a marketing department issue. It's not. Every lender needs to be able to write a compelling letter to the different sectors she has targeted. Every development officer needs to know how to write strong letters to potential members and members that result in more accounts.

Less than 5 percent of the mail delivered today is personalized mail. If a letter comes in the mail that has a stamp and our name typed or better yet hand-written on the envelope, we are thrilled that there is something in the mail we actually want to open.

It's the same with your members. Your members get hit with postcards, brochures, and hundreds of mailing label pieces. So when a letter is personalized, written on your stationery, and composed to help them solve a problem they have, you've got a great chance of actually getting them to take some action.

Imagine a small firm that is doing some international business getting a letter that starts with the headline, "How will you protect your business from currency fluctuations that could crush your bottom line?" If you offered a FREE report on services that would protect them from that concern and offered to take the management of that out of their hands, do you think they would call for it? Absolutely!

Direct-mail letters allow you to do one-to-one marketing to hundreds of niche markets, with each letter approaching a specific problem of that group and a solution you can provide.

Instead of buying a billboard that reads, "Hey, we're great…and we're your hometown credit union!" invest those dollars in a mail campaign to thousands of tightly niched sectors where you have a proven history of success. Give them the detailed solution that they're looking for.

Here is an example with a tightly woven targeted message that would be more effective than a generic message:

> For middle class investors: How to increase your long-term returns with an investing process that decreases the volatility of your account.

Composing and Customizing Your Sales Letter

Now it's time to consider the contents of your direct mail letter. How often do consumers receive personalized letters from their credit unions offering them advice? The chances are slim to none. Most receive a canned, glossy brochure stuffed into their monthly statements that they never read. So why not stand out from your competition by running a direct mail campaign that's filled with useful information and genuine offers of help? How about doing this *without asking for anything in return?*

> **Founding Concept: Give and You Shall Receive.**

This type of direct marketing campaign will definitely get attention — and results. In fact, Dr. Cialdini, the author of *Influence*, has proven that when people are given something for free, they feel an overwhelming need to return the favor. (More information on Dr. Cialdini's findings will follow later in this chapter.)

Sample "Giving Freely" Ideas

- What if your trusted members received a monthly personalized letter that relayed relevant tax advice?

- What if you offered free classes each month in your lobby on wealth building and protection ideas?
- What if you gave a free financial planning workbook to each member?

Do you think these direct mail campaigns would compel the audience to do more business with you? Yes, definitely!

> **Information is the most valued gift you can give FREELY!**

Make recipients an offer they can't refuse.

Let's face it: most credit union people aren't great writers. Perhaps running a credit union is a left-brain function, whereas writing is a right-brain function. Who knows? Even if you're not a Hemingway, you can still compose a killer direct marketing letter, guaranteed!

How? Follow the **AIDA formula** below and enlist a little help from local copywriting experts.

> **A — Attention:** You have only seconds to grab the reader and pull that person into your message. We live in a world of instant messages and instant responses. Answering yes or no takes only seconds. If you don't quickly catch the reader's attention by standing out from the other mail they receive, your direct mail campaign will be tossed in the circular file of defeat never to return again. You MUST find a way to grab their **attention**.
>
> **I — Interest:** WIIFM! Next, you need to create **interest** by focusing on benefits. Most credit unions, if they do

any direct mail at all, tend to list features but never answer the only question in which their readers are interested: "What's In It For Me?" Let's face it; we're all a lot more self-consumed than we'd like to admit. Involve readers emotionally in your information. If you are passionate about what you have to give them because it will BENEFIT them, let them know this. They will respond as a result.

D — Desire: After establishing interest, you now need to instill **desire**. Offering a special bonus, providing guarantees, or using member testimonials are great ways to create desire and ensure quick responses from your mailing's recipients. Remember your survey! You know what strokes their hot buttons, what makes them want what you have to offer, and what makes them respond to the way you offer it to them. So use this information to appeal to them.

A — Action: Finally, you want to move readers into **action**. Don't just assume they'll respond to your offer: ASK them to call or come in. Also create a sense of urgency. Give a limited time offer. People nowadays are constantly bombarded by offers, so their memory tends to be very short. Make sure your phone number stands out, as well as **"Call for FREE."** Letting them know they can call an 800 or local number and gain some valuable free information is not threatening, and it is the best response mechanism known in direct mail advertising. Ask them to come into the credit union at a certain time on a certain day for something free as well.

Writing Your Sales Letter

Okay, so now you have your AIDA action plan and are ready to start writing.

Where to begin?

It all starts with a headline. To write a KILLER headline you must do two things.

1. Attract your audience's attention while they're sorting through their mail.

2. Break into the conversation that's already going on inside their head.

Sounds simple? Well, it is.

Just like in regular conversations, you sometimes need to say, "Hey, pay attention! You really need to hear this!" The same is true for your direct marketing letters. The magic really happens when you finally understand your readers' main concern and what they'd like done about it. If you can discover this and compose a headline that makes readers believe you can help them overcome it, you're sure to get their full, undivided attention.

Advertising genius David Ogilvy says:

> "On the average, five times as many people read headlines versus body copy. It follows that, unless your headline sells your product, you have wasted 90 percent of your money."

John Caples contends:

> "If you have a good headline, you have a good ad. Any competent writer can write copy. But if you have a poor headline, you are licked before you start. Your copy will not be read . . .. Spend hours writing headlines — or days if necessary."

So, what does your headline need to do?
1. **Speak only to your potential member.** For example, "Members: Discover How You Can Save More Time While Getting Higher Returns on Your Accounts."
2. **Offer the greatest possible benefit to the reader.**
3. **Compel the reader to keep reading.** You want the readers to stay curious about how the benefits will help that person.
4. **Suggest a fast and easy way for the reader to get the benefit** — but make sure it's believable.
5. **Use highly effective grabber words.** Studies have shown the following words are highly effective in headlines.

The Three Most Compelling Words:
You
How
New

Next Most Compelling Words:
How to

Additional Top 20 Attention-Grabbing Words:

Amazing	At Last	Which
Announcing	Sale	Only
Breakthrough	Protect	Yes
Just	Now	Here
Discover	Astonishing	Why
Free	Introducing	This
New	Secrets of	

Your Powerful Sales Letter Body Copy

Of course, you can combine these words for a greater effect:

■■

Announcing New FREE Special Report . . .
Seven Amazing Secrets of the Rich that You, too, Can Use to Protect Your Wealth and Simplify Your Life

■■

How to Protect Your Business from Fraud: Astonishing Facts You Must Know!

■■

At Last: You Can Discover How to Break Through to
Financial Freedom!

                                                 Here's How . . .

■■

Forget what your teacher taught you because great copy is not always great English. Here are some new rules to learn:

1. **Write one-to-one.** Visualize the ideal reader for your letter and write directly to that one person! Although your letter may be going out to thousands, using the words "you" and "your" will make it feel like you're speaking directly to the person reading the letter.

Example:

A friend of mine received a letter from a president of a financial services institution. She had never received a letter from a financial institution's president before. She opened it because it said president on the outside of the envelope.

The headline read: **Announcing Your College Fund Resource**

The letter began: Dear Ms. ----, (her first and last name).

The first sentence read: As Joy's mom . . .

She glanced at the signature, and it was in blue ink, personally signed by the president, and he had written her a handwritten P.S.:

"Wishing you the best in all you do. Hope this information will make some of your and your daughter's dreams come true. Come into my institution and ask for the college open-door package we have prepared for you and your daughter. Do this any time before

Friday, Feb. 28, and also receive a personal gift: a free special report my financial institution has prepared for you about how you can beat rising college costs over the next four years.

(Of course, my friend had a senior in high school who was researching colleges. She was a single parent.)

Did this president handwrite his signature and the postscript note?

No, but it sure seemed that way.

Was that P. S. note effective?

Yes, because the financial institution had done its research and was mailing to parents of high school seniors about the financial needs of college students away from home.

What made it more special was the personalized name. Though it's not necessary to use the person's name, it does add a personal touch.

Most importantly, the letter gave solutions to many financial concerns regarding students away from home for the first time. These included a system of receiving instant money when the student runs out, a forewarning about credit card offers to college kids, a way to avoid credit card debt, and numerous other issues about finances and handling money for college kids. No mention was made about loans for tuition in that letter, but you can be certain that this was the major reason the organization's marketing team had selected the mailing list and composed the letter and information packet as they did.

Was this successful? Yes. The mother and daughter opened a joint account, used the financial institution to secure college loans, and even signed up for a credit card with first-year, second-year, third-year and fourth-year limits that increased to $5,000, and then to $25,000 after graduation. A few years later when my friend started her own business, she turned to that same institution to take out business loans.

See what one-to-one communication can do?

2. **Never end a sentence at the end of the page.** In fact, make sure the last sentence on each page is so compelling that it forces the reader to turn the page.

3. **Break up your copy.** Put it into easy-to-read, bite-size chunks by using lots of indentations, subheads, and short paragraphs. (Note: It's perfectly fine to use just one, two, or three sentences per paragraph. In fact, mini paragraphs are usually more effective in advertising copy.)

4. **Convey your passion.** Your enthusiasm, or noticeable lack thereof, will make a huge difference in the response your letter receives.

5. **Use bullets** •
    Italicizing
    Bolding
    boxes ■
    underlining
    other means of formatting to keep readers interested.

6. **Use active, not passive, verbs.** Bring your copy into the present tense by avoiding past-tense qualifiers like "was," "were," "had," or "has been." Again, this will make your

letter seem like it's speaking directly to each reader — not to thousands of them.

The Easy-to-Use, Can't-Go-Wrong, Result-Generating, Three-Step Formula to Writing a Great and Compelling Letter

---

7. **Good copywriters know the magic formula to creating sales letters that get results:**

   - **Identify the reader's problem.**
   - **Accentuate the negatives.**
   - **Offer a solution.**

Some call this type of writing the "problem-agitation-solution" formula. It works because most people make purchasing decisions to avoid pain and gain pleasure. Use this powerful insight to your advantage!

1. Identify the member's pain.

Example:

> "With hundreds to thousands of OPTIONS, how do you know you're not paying too much in closing costs and making a wrong choice based on your unique situation?"

2. Create a desire to overcome this pain by engaging on the member's emotions.

Example:

> "Rates don't tell the whole story of the true cost. You can call hundreds of financial institutions and shop the rates, but nine times out of ten they will only quote you the rate. How will you know how to get the best value that saves you the most money over time when the structure of the loan and the closing costs make such a huge impact on your REAL cost?"

3. Deliver the Solution.

Example:

> "Finally, there's an easy-to-use process that identifies your exact needs and directs you to the best alternatives that could save you thousands of dollars! Read on to learn how."

This formula can't miss. Try it.

The P.S.

After the headline, the P.S. section is the second most read part of any direct mail letter. Use this area to reiterate your benefit for buying and/or the reason they need to buy now. Give a date and offer something free if they respond by that date.

Scarcity

A primary purchasing motivator is scarcity. To avoid missing out or paying a higher price, people tend to make purchasing decisions faster if they're afraid they'll miss the "special" discount being offered for a "limited time."

Examples:

> "Sign up for our small-business seminar while you still can. Only 13 seats remain."
>
> "Only the first 50 people to sign up for our upgraded checking program will receive Internet bill pay services for FREE!!! So act now."

4. Give a Good Reason to Buy.

Dr. Robert Cialdini is an Arizona-based sociology professor who wrote the best-selling book *Influence: The Psychology of Persuasion*. This work instructs readers on how to influence others and get them to do what you want them to do. I highly suggest reading it.

One of his key insights is that people like to have reasons for doing the things they do. In one of his experiments, he approached people using a copy machine and said, "Excuse me. May I use the Xerox machine?" This approach received a 60 percent success rate.

In his second approach he said, "Excuse me. I have five pages. May I use the Xerox machine *because* I'm in a rush?" This tactic was successful 94 percent of the time.

In his final approach he said, "Excuse me. I have five pages. May I use the Xerox machine *because* I have to make some copies?"

No reason was mentioned — he just used the word "because." Remarkably 93 percent of the time, the person using the copy machine said yes.

As you can see, giving a reason or just saying "because" holds a lot of weight in getting what you want. So include it in your direct mail letters.

Examples:

> "We want you to attend this seminar *because* we want to make sure all of our small business members are as successful with their employee recruitment as possible."
>
> "Why can we offer you this unbelievably inexpensive offer? *Because* we know that once you open a premier checking account with us, you will see how much better service with us really is and you'll bring over the rest of your business."

Now that you have a great letter…

Create a letter campaign. It's more valuable to mail to the same smaller list six times than it is to mail to a larger list once. Create a series of letters to go to the same market. Each of us buys on the day we're ready. When the emotion hits and your letter hits that same day, you'll get a new member.

When strategizing your mail campaign, plan the timing based on when people buy. According to Gary Halbert, renowned direct-mail expert, the most effective mail of the year is received the first week in January, followed by the next eleven weeks. Summer is a very ineffective time for mail campaigns. The warmer the temperature, the more lethargic the buying process.

Of course, if your mailing has to do with college financing, timing is every thing.

Choose a mail house carefully. You don't want a postal meter stamping your mail and giving the impression it's not personal. So when you ask the mail house to put on stamps, note that stamps are like cash. You probably wouldn't ask your tellers to handle thousands of dollars of cash with no accountability. Nor should you let the employees of the direct mail company not account for each mailing piece. Direct mail specialists have measured from a 10 to 40 percent increase in response rates when they actually took the mail pieces to the post office themselves. Hmmm.... I hate to believe that's true. But until that statistic changes, it looks like you'll want to do the trip to the post office yourself.

A good sales letter can take the message of your top salesperson (the objections they hear and how they overcome them) and leverage the genius of that sales master thousands of times beyond his or her human capacity to call on members.

It can be filled with bulleted lists of benefits that compel the reader to take action.

Hire a great copywriter to write your letters. The power of high-impact words that tell the story and elicit the emotional response — the only one that causes people to take action — can double or triple sales within days.

Direct mail is the best bang-for-your-buck tactic you have. Although it takes more talent and creativity than a newspaper ad, the results speak for themselves.

Strategy 7: Change Your Strategy.

Go back over Chapter 4 and review strategy. It is fundamental to effective marketing. If you do not have a growth strategy for every area of your credit union, then you will never be able to implement them successfully. You need specific strategies for each aspect of your marketing.

Questions to Answer Regarding Your Marketing Plan

The most effective marketing plans are highly focused. Before writing ten pages, write one sentence to describe each of the following seven areas. This will help you create a clear, concise, and compelling marketing plan.

1. What is the purpose of your strategy?
2. What are your competitive advantages and how will you use them to accomplish your strategy?
3. Who is your target market?
4. What mediums and tactics will you use to reach your target market?
5. What is your niche or niches?
6. What is the identity you're trying to convey?
7. What percentage of your gross revenues will you use for your marketing budget?

Most credit unions promote their image (such as being a "friendly credit union") even though that is far from how members actually find them. And when a credit union's image doesn't match a member's experience, that member becomes distrustful, and often resentful, of that organization.

As far as marketing budgets, most credit unions forget their true purpose: improving business. They often see budgets devoted to marketing as a waste of money rather than as an investment.

Example:

> Several years ago a financial institution's management team asked us to work with them, but not until the next year because they had not scheduled it in their current year's budget.
>
> A few weeks later, their competitor also contacted us to help them out, but they wanted to start immediately. Of course, I called the first institution and, since they contacted us first, gave them the opportunity to start our partnership now. (Since we never work with competing financial institutions, they would either have to start now or forgo a relationship entirely.) Unfortunately, they decided to stick to their predetermined budget and forgo the investment.
>
> I'll bet you can guess what happened next. Within six months, the competitor, following our templates, took money out of the first institution so quickly they couldn't turn off the faucet of run-off. And they are still experiencing it today.

My point? Make your marketing decisions based on need and timing. If this means adjusting the budget you set 18 months ago, so be it. Why pass up on any opportunities for growing your business?

Okay, I'm sure you're now thinking, "Yes, I can see your logic, but times are really tough right now. Can we really afford to expand our marketing activities in today's economy?"

Reasons to Market

The real question is, can you afford not to market?

Consider the following:

1. **Marketing builds your identity.** If you stop, your members will lose confidence in your stability.

2. **Marketing improves your member retention.** When your members cease to hear from you, they assume you don't care anymore and they become more receptive to your competition.

3. **Marketing helps you attract new members.** Nearly 21 percent of Americans change residences each year. Nearly 6 million get married each year. Without continual marketing, you'll miss out on these opportunities.

4. **Marketing keeps your competitors in check.** Chances are, your competition is growing — fast. And you can bet they're ready and waiting to take advantage of the opportunities you miss when you slow down or stop your marketing efforts.

5. **Marketing is paramount to your growth and survival.** Ever heard the expression "out of sight, out of mind"? This is true for your current and potential members. When you stop marketing to them, they'll forget you.

6. **Marketing improves morale.** Employees want to be part of a successful team. And the more you market, the more successful your credit union appears and, eventually, becomes.

7. **Marketing gives you an edge.** A bad economy is a great time for marketing-minded organizations to up their promotions and pull away from competitors (who will probably cut back on their advertising). Every economic situation has winners and losers, and tough times require more focused and consistent marketing efforts.

Summary

Excellent marketing is more a function of consistent creativity than of big budgets. Financial organizations that differentiate themselves in a way that is meaningful to their target members will make life very difficult for financial institutions still using the "hometown" or "friendly people" approach. Why? Today's consumers have become far too sophisticated for rhetoric and empty promises.

Action Plan for Implementing Strategies in Chapter 5

Action to Take	Responsible Person	Results	Start Date	Target Date

Benefits

6 Breakthrough Sales

How to Break Through
The "Order Taking" Habit for Good

It happens all day long, every single day in almost every credit union. The phone rings. A well-meaning staff person answers politely. The dialogue begins:

Inquirer: "What are your mortgage rates?"

(The misguided but polite staffer proceeds to recite the day's rate list.)

Inquirer: "Thank you."

Misguided but polite staffer: "Thank you."

Click: Conversation ends.

No attempt has been made to understand the reasons behind the rate inquiry. Nor has any attempt been made to connect with the prospective member and his or her needs.

We make it a standard practice to dismiss them over and over again.

Why?

We don't train our people to know what to do to convert the conversation from one of rates to one of value. This is also true in the deposit-gathering area, an area that has been a struggle for many credit unions.

In researching several hundred banks and credit unions in Wisconsin, we found that 95 percent of rate shoppers were merely told a rate, and the institution made no attempt to inquire about the nature of the caller's needs and no attempt to help the caller meet those needs.

What is wrong with this picture?

In both of these research studies, the caller received no added value beyond the recital of rates — a task that can be more efficiently accomplished on the Internet.

The mortgage inquirer received no guidance and was allowed to continue on a quest for rate and rate alone. We all know that the lowest rate might not be associated with the mortgage instrument that is best suited to meet the caller's needs.

Furthermore, the caller gained no knowledge of the different closing cost options and how much money can be saved by choosing the right instrument.

No *help* was given.

So what are potential members forced to do?

They move on to the next financial institution to inquire about rates and gain no further knowledge about how to make a good decision.

Imagine the relationship building that could occur if instead these callers were to hear a message like this:

> "We want to make sure you get the best possible mortgage for your needs. Rate is only one part of the true costs, so let me coach you on how to get the least expensive mortgage based on your needs."

This rarely happens. There is often no relationship development so that callers would feel safe sharing confidential financial information. They do not come away from the call with a sense of trust, nor are they assured that they will be counseled wisely during what may be the biggest financial decision they'll make in their lifetime.

At Some Point We Have to Accept the Truth

It is no accident that the banking and credit union industries have lost 85 percent of the market share over the last 100 years. Something is substantially wrong with this picture!

Even the basics of handling rate inquiries, a place where potential members are practically waving a flag that says, "Please, let me give you my money," are missed by the best intentioned of employees who enthusiastically quote the rates.

In this scenario, you can only lose. Either you cave into this mentality of rate-oriented selling at the expense of your bottom line, or you protect your margin with higher rates — and fail to win the favor of what you believe to be a rate-oriented audience.

Is there another way?

Absolutely.

Your Solution

Create a quantifiable and replicable system that is guaranteed to help you win more members.

Credit unions are big on systems. Can you imagine a credit union not having a system for balancing a drawer? Or a credit union that has such a system but no one bothers to monitor whether tellers follow it? In such an environment, supervisors would likely develop a rather laissez-faire attitude: "Oh, don't worry your pretty little head. If you're busy, or tired, don't worry about balancing your drawer today. It's not that important."

This seems ludicrous. What credit union wouldn't have a system for balancing drawers? Credit unions have systems for processing loans, systems for handling loan payments, systems for collecting tax deposits, and hundreds of other systems over which the management team would absolutely go ballistic if their people didn't follow them to the letter.

The systems are monitored each day. Exceptions are reported immediately. Corrective actions are taken. Following these systems is an expectation for employment.

Now, contrast this to the sales management philosophy of most credit union management teams. It plays out something like this:

> The senior management team creates a strategic plan which says that developing the sales culture is their primary concern. With hands on hips, they say, "We're serious."
>
> Then they go back and send a memo to their people, saying, "And, by the way, we want you to sell now."
>
> Whew, that hard work is done.
>
> And then it happens — the realization that now not only are the sales figures not looking any better, but the staff is cranky and whining in the break room about how they are NOT going to lower themselves to be "pushy" salespeople and management will just have to deal with it!

This could be called the "create an expectation that no one can fulfill and then watch morale go right down the tubes when it doesn't happen" approach to managing. Add to that the fit management will throw in anger when their people aren't performing.

Next, things get worse. When sales aren't increasing, the credit union brings in a trainer who teaches old-school features and benefits, and all those attending smile and nod — and nothing changes.

Things get terrible. Sales campaigns are created with sales quotas and tellers are selling products by being pushy.

"How would you like to open a Christmas account today?" chirps the well-meaning young teller to the high-powered executive with massive wealth — who also just happens to be Jewish. Clearly, he's not impressed!

Another employee holds out the sales brochure in front of a new member's face, recites all fourteen different types of checking accounts, and then, with a cheerful voice, asks, "So, which one do you want?"

Many credit unions have made false starts in generating a sales culture by first creating goals and then incentives for meeting those goals. These should be the last steps after guiding employees through a powerfully effective sales process that helps them realize they're doing a better job of HELPING people — not pushing products.

What's the point?

If you don't have detailed and strategic systems in place for all the areas of sales and referrals within each department, the chances of getting significant sales increases are slim to none.

What Thinking Style Are You?

Several years ago I heard of a psychologist who came up with the concept of thinking styles. According to this person, 2 percent of all people are conceptual thinkers, 18 percent are strategic thinkers, and the remaining 80 percent are operational thinkers.

What does this mean for you? Generally, at least 80 percent of the people who work in your credit union will be operational thinkers. Actually, it will probably be a higher percentage, as people who possess this thinking style are attracted to credit unions. They have the kind of personality such that, if you tell them step by step how to do something, they will do it. They won't be able to conceptualize the direction, nor will they be able to create the system.

On the other hand, once a system is developed, operational thinkers are great at following it. In fact, they love to know that all they have to do is follow a great system, and it gives them a sense of success.

Many credit union leaders, on the other hand, tend to be strategic and conceptual thinkers. They attempt to disseminate information by simply saying they want something done right, without any explanation of how it should be done.

Clearly, credit union leaders must expand beyond their conceptual thinking model and create the systems that will ensure "buy-in" and improved morale among their employees — and ensure their organization's growth.

Problem: No One in the Credit Union Is Designated to Create and Audit Sales Systems

Operational managers and compliance officers make sure a system is both devised and followed for every technical aspect of a credit union. One would never think of doing anything but be in the strictest compliance in those areas. If there is a problem, management is up in arms.

Unfortunately, most credit unions have no one creating a system for sales. Just as important, they have no one in charge of auditing sales and referral systems to make sure every person is in 100 percent compliance. Need I even mention, then, that there are no consequences to not following the sales system?

Needed Sales Systems

What systems should you create?

Not only do you need systems for rate inquiries in EVERY functional area within your credit union, you also need systems for referrals, sales calls, and ongoing relationships with current members.

Rate Inquiry Systems

> Many years ago when I was starting a new financial organization, I interviewed and hired my staff in a little rented room close to our facility that was under construction. As most building projects go, ours was not meeting the completion deadline. So on the day of our opening, due to the fact that the carpet had been laid only the day before, our furniture had not yet arrived. Throughout the building, we sat on plastic chairs with our phones on the floor and our work in our laps. It was a Kodak moment!
>
> On that first morning, a woman I'll call Julie (to protect the guilty), whom I had hired from a competitor, was the first one to answer an incoming phone call. She reached down from her plastic chair for the phone on the floor.

It shocked me that the phone rang within minutes of our opening. We hadn't even told anybody we were there yet because we weren't quite ready for the public to come in and evaluate us; and yet, someone had found our number and had decided to shop our rates.

After the call, I went to Julie and asked, "Who was that?"

"Someone wanting to know our CD rates."

"Really! I'm just amazed they found us. How did it go?"

"Well, they wanted the rates, so I reached for the rate sheet and gave them the rates."

"And then what happened?"

"They thanked me for the help and hung up."

I sat in shock. Here was our first potential customer and we let him slip right through our fingers — as if we could afford to let any customer that came our way just keep shopping.

Julie had the best sense of humor I had run into in years, so I knew I could play with her. I felt compelled to help her understand why she needed to perform differently from the way she had become accustomed to in her previous employment.

"Julie, there's a concept I want to share with you. We are a financial business. We need MONEY. When someone calls in for rates, it usually means they have MONEY. Next time, when they call in, make sure to ask them for their MONEY."

As unrefined as that system was, it worked. I heard her from that point on saying, "Gee, we'd really like to do business with you. We'd take very good care of you." And, miraculously, the business came in.

That was not all . . .

Several weeks later, I thought there were still too many rate shoppers who, despite Julie's and others' offers to do business, hung up to continue their rate shopping. It occurred to me there must be a way to stop the rate shoppers in their tracks and earn their business instantly.

So we decided to script a few questions we could ask people when they called to break their preoccupation with just a quick rate quote and intrigue them with the value we could add.

That system of scripted questions my team began back then has since been implemented in my work with hundreds of financial organizations — with instantaneous and measurable success. The example below is just one of many success stories resulting from the use of such a system.

One Success Story

A CEO from a $150 million financial organization called me one day and said, "Roxanne, you're not going to believe what happened. I was down in the new accounts area one day when I noticed that the entire new accounts staff was away from their desks and the phone was ringing. I can't stand the sound of an unanswered phone, so I leaped over the desk to answer the phone."

It turns out the caller wanted to know his company's CD rates. The CEO reached for the "orange sheet" his staff had developed in one of the training sessions I had done for them six months earlier, and he began to read the questions as scripted.

"Sure," he said. "While I get those rates for you, let me ask you a few questions to make sure I recommend only the types of investments that give you the results you are looking for." And he made his way down the list of questions.

"Roxanne, I just couldn't wait to call to tell you what happened next. The woman who called initially told me she wanted a $5,000 CD. **After following your questions, we picked up an $85,000 CD and half a million dollar trust account. THIS STUFF REALLY WORKS!"**

The reason it works is that the best possible thing you can do to improve your sales is to be legitimately more interested in the needs and wants of your current members and future ones. By asking them solid and thoughtful questions, it allows them to dig deeper into their wants and needs, prompting them to consider options they might otherwise never have thought about.

Even more importantly, members feel they have finally found someone who actually cares about them and their needs. Suddenly, the value placed on "rate" as a decision criterion has lost its luster. They feel they can't afford NOT to do business with you.

First Things First

Rate inquiries are the low-hanging fruit. When I first work with a financial institution, we begin by systematizing the rate inquiries in every department.

> The first financial organization I ever advised was a little $40 million institution that hadn't grown in four years. Within two weeks they had picked up $2.5 million!

Most credit unions attempting to grow start with an advertising campaign and other low-return investments. Why push water up a hill? It's a whole lot easier to capture a larger percentage of people who are already driving to your credit union, are in a buying mood, and possess the resources to buy, than to "throw it against the wall and see what sticks" with a wide-spanning and expensive marketing campaign.

Steps in a Profitable Rate Inquiry Process

Step #1: Break the Preoccupation.

What is the preoccupation of every rate shopper?

Yes, that's right: The rate.

And yet we know that, when researched, most people are willing to accept 40 basis points less than a competitor's rate with little resistance at all. People will accept a lower rate when they are substantially convinced of the **value** that goes along with it. This could include the special services they receive at your credit union that they wouldn't receive at your competitor's financial institution. After all, wouldn't you pay more for a Mercedes than you would for a Yugo?

First Question Sample:

On the form you use for ALL mortgage rate inquiries, the first question should read something like the following:

> "Are you looking for the best rate, or the best value? There are many costs and approaches to mortgages,

and it's very common for the best rate not to be the best value."

or

"Before I present a whole list of CD rates to you, I'd like to ask you a few questions to find out how we can make sure we're helping you make the best investment decision for the long run and maximizing your return. Would that be okay with you?"

It's hard for anyone to say, "Hey, I'm just rate shopping" after that display of commitment to finding them the best value AND protecting them from all those others they've shopped with who DIDN'T look out for them in this way.

Breaking the preoccupation with rate then gives you the opportunity to ask if you may present some more questions to better understand what the caller needs and wants.

Step #2: Find Out the Needs.

It is only legitimate that you ask questions about peoples' finances if you are to advise them and help them with their finances. Yet most credit union employees are appalled at the idea of asking people these questions. The funny thing is, they often already know more about the member's finances than the member's mother, father, best friend, and, sometimes, even his or her spouse!

Think about how you would feel if you went to your physician and were met at the door by a doctor with a prescription pad in hand who said, "We're trying this new program. We're just prescribing penicillin to our clients today. It's the special! That will be $100, and thanks for coming!"

People's financial health is often as important to them as their physical health. That's why so many people have left credit unions that have seemed indifferent to their needs. They want someone to give them their yearly physical. They are far too busy to educate themselves on the best options; they would love someone to hold their hand and advise them on the best solutions, as opposed to someone handing over a brochure and asking, "So, what do you want?"

Step # 3: Use Situational Questions.

Next, you ask the "situational" questions to find out what it is that the member is really trying to do. These are "safe" questions without much depth.

Examples of Situational Questions:

"How long do you intend to live in this house?"

"What's important to you in a mortgage?"

"What did you like about your last mortgage?"

"What did you dislike?"

"What's most important to you: getting the lowest payment or paying it off quickly?"

In contrast to situational questions, lenders often start with jargon and completely miss selling opportunities, all the while confusing their prospects into indecision.

Example of a Jargon-laced INEFFECTIVE question:

"What kind of mortgage do you want?"

How could they possibly know what's best? They don't sit up at night reading about the loan options and how to present value the flow of payments so they can find the break-even point to see if they're better off paying a higher rate or more in points. That's why you're there to help!

Example of confusing credit union–lingo INEFFECTIVE questions:

> "Did you want a conventional?" (No, I think I'll have a radical.)

> "Are you looking for a jumbo?" (No, but you just made me feel like Dumbo, since I couldn't possibly know what the new limits for a jumbo are unless I've shopped elsewhere, which I now feel like doing.)

The jargon in the mortgage industry is overwhelming to even an experienced homebuyer. The use of technical verbiage creates a big problem. People are made to feel stupid when they don't know what you are talking about. **And people don't buy from people who make them feel stupid.**

Another problem is that this approach forces members to make choices about products they do not understand or which are not the best for their needs. You haven't counseled them. You've only frustrated them.

Without writing down good situational questions, the temptation to ask poor questions is extremely high. Once a really poor question gets out, you lose any opportunity to gain back credibility. One bad question can make rejuvenating the deal an impossible feat. That's why . . .

> **ALL QUESTIONS** should be written on a form that is used incessantly so there is no chance of sticking the proverbial foot in one's mouth at the least opportune time.

Step # 4: Ask Positioning Questions.

Not only do you want to know what your members' needs are so that you can make excellent recommendations, **you also want them to understand how you differ from the competition and why that is important for them.** Don't assume they know.

Many credit union associates approach this by doing a dog-and-pony show in which they "tell, tell, tell" and the member tunes out.

The only opinion people won't argue with is their own. So the key is to help them understand why your differences are the logical solution for them. Consequently, **you allow them to tell YOU why you're the right choice.**

Do this by asking a question that implies why the answer is important.

How do you do this?

Start by listing the differences you have that are important to them, and then build questions around those differences so that their answer will tell you why they want to do business with you.

Examples:

Your Advantage: Open seven days a week.

Question: How important is it to you to do business with a credit union that is open seven days a week as opposed to the inconvenience of having to leave work early to do your financial business?

Your Advantage: Personal service where staff knows members' names.

Question: How important is it to you to do business with a financial institution where people know your name?

Your Advantage: The most mortgage options of any financial institution in town.

Question: How important is it to you to do business with a financial institution that has the most mortgage products, assuring you not only a competitive rate, but the best possible customized solution for your specific needs?

The Importance of Using How Questions

Notice that I began each question with "How." This forces the prospect to talk. They can't answer with "yes" or "no." They must engage. And if some particular thing is not that important, that's okay too. You simply go on to another question to find out what **is** important.

Selling Themselves

Once they start answering with absolute resolution that one or more of your benefits is very important to them, they have just sold themselves on you. They also have a sales pitch they have perfected that they hopefully will use to tell their friends, family, and neighbors about you!

This is the part where you help them understand that they found exactly the right place for them; they understand your uniqueness and why it's very valuable to them — even more valuable than getting a better rate with one of your competitors.

Analyze Your Strengths and Weaknesses and Those of Your Competitors, and Then Ask the Right Questions

To build this into the system, start by analyzing your strengths and the weaknesses of your competitors. Then, shape questions around those strengths so that instead of just telling your member why you're great, you get them to tell you why your difference is very important to them.

The result? members tell you why they need to do business with you.

Examples of Selected Benefits and the Questions That Should Be Built into Your Sales System:

> **Benefit:** Quick processing . . .
>
> **Question:** How important is it to you that you work with a mortgage lender that can approve and process your loan in a fraction of the time it takes other lenders, thus ensuring that you don't miss out on the perfect house?
>
> **Benefit:** Low closing costs . . .

Question: How important is it to you to work with a lender that doesn't have the substantial front-end closing costs that dramatically increase the real cost of your mortgage, especially if you don't actually end up staying in the house for 30 years?

Benefit: Weekly exception reporting . . .

Question: How important is it to you to have detailed weekly reporting of all the necessary documents for the closing, so you won't have a nightmare experience at the closing?

Benefit: One loan officer from application to closing . . .

Question: How important is it to you to have one person hold your hand from the beginning to the closing of this process to make sure everything goes smoothly, as opposed to many mortgage processes where they just take your application and leave you to fend for yourself at the closing or shift you from person to person?

Benefit: The largest selection of offerings . . .

Question: How important is it to you to work with a lender that has the largest selection of mortgage offerings so you can make sure you are getting the best possible mortgage for you and your needs?

By clearly defining your strengths and shaping the conversation in this way, the member will tell you what they want and why they want it. **They are thrilled to choose you because they just talked themselves into it!**

If your positioning questions are not written down, the chances of you and your employees asking them well are extremely slim. And the chances of the questions getting worse over time are huge.

> **Write down your questions!**

Step #5: Repeat.

Based on what they told you . . .

1) Restate your understanding of what is important regarding the member's needs and what they desire in a financial institutional relationship.

2) Ask for clarification by having the member confirm that what you heard was exactly right.

Slow down and wait for the right opportunity to finalize the sale.

Salespeople get excited when everything seems to be going their way. Therefore, they want to start selling. Resist the temptation until this step is handled.

People desperately want to be understood. They want to know that you not only understand them, but that you care. So take the time to let them know they weren't just spewing words on deaf ears.

> **Take the time to show you care.**

Start this step with summary and "I understand you" statements:

"So, if I heard correctly, you said …

" … you're planning on living in the house forever, but that's what you thought when you bought the last two homes in which you lived for only three years each. Now you don't want to pay too much for a long-term rate."

"… you are very concerned about stretching yourself too thin, but you would like to pay down extra principle when you have excess cash."

"… you think rates might go down some more so you want the flexibility to change your rate without additional closing costs IF that were to happen in the future."

Then, *LISTEN*.

Find out what you missed and acknowledge those items before moving onto the next step.

Step #6: Make Suggestions.

Taking what you have learned about the member's situation, suggest different options and financial solutions.

Those suggestions should be along the lines of . . .

"And I'd love to make your life less complicated and take care of ALL of your financial business in one place to save you time. Here's what I recommend we do."

This step should start out by letting them know that you are about to make suggestions based on what *they* said was important.

EXTRAORDINARY CREDIT UNIONS

The wording should go something like this . . .

> "Based on what you have told me, I'm going to recommend . . . (suggest a product or service that fits their needs)."

You should end with something like . . .

> "...because this would help you _____ (describe the need they expressed)."

Step #7: Ask for the Order.

Fear of Facing No's and Rejection

This is the part that scares most people. The reason is because most sales staff use the wrong approach from the start. If you haven't done an excellent job of finding out what the member needs, that member will most likely be resistant when you start to push in a direction that isn't right for them.

Yes, this IS the step people tend to forget. Perhaps it isn't forgotten at all. Perhaps it's just too scary to put oneself in the position of being rejected.

Eliminating No's and Rejection

Rejection comes when we present something that isn't right. The only way to do that is to do steps one through six poorly. If, on the other hand, you've followed your carefully scripted powerful questions, your members will have nothing to reject. They will willingly become your members.

Asking for the order isn't about coercing someone to give you their money with no regard for their needs. **It's about caring so much about their needs that you feel compelled to help them right away.**

The "old school" of sales training called this "closing." They taught it at the time when the arm wrestling begins. Let me suggest that if arm wrestling takes place, you've clearly done an extremely poor job of the first steps, and the member will probably want to run and not come back.

The ONLY Valid Closing Question

The only closing question that should ever roll off your tongue in an extremely nonintimidating way is:

> **"Do you have any further questions or would you like to get started?"**

That's it. Easy. Simple. Clean. Not manipulative. And extremely helpful. If they have questions, you answer the questions and then find out if they want to move ahead. If they say they don't want to move ahead, they'll probably feel inclined to want to tell you why. At this point you should set out to immediately rectify the situation.

Step #8: Thank them for the order and assure them you will take good care of them and that you intend to help them with all of their financial concerns.

Overcoming Buyer's Remorse

Immediately after buying, most buyers have a twinge of buyer's remorse. They wonder if they made the right choice or if they may have misunderstood something or some intent.

Your job is to make sure they know you will take care of them no matter what their questions or challenges are.

I had been a commercial lender for almost four years before I had even taken out a loan myself. It was an awakening.

The organization I worked for didn't make the kind of loan I was looking for, so I went to a financial institution that a friend had referred me to. After signing the mound of paperwork that all seemed to say, "You mess up and you're hung up by your toenails with chicken wire," I experienced a sense of panic. I had a sick feeling in my stomach. I was inundated with melodramatic thoughts of what would happen if I became ill or disabled or if a recession knocked my revenues down so substantially I couldn't make payments. Stretched any further, I could have been able to envision myself living in a cardboard box on Main Street!

As if reading my mind about how surprised I was to be scared at this moment — a moment when I had a new insight about what it felt like for MY clients to be on this side of the desk — the loan officer stood up, walked around his desk, reached to shake my hand, and said,

"Don't worry. We'll take really good care of you."

Suddenly, I felt much calmer. My mind immediately raced to the thought of a friend of mine I wanted to refer to this loan officer, as my other friend had referred me.

Overcoming the Financial Service Industry's Reputation

Financial services have gotten a bad reputation because of the history of some financial institutions treating their members as subservient people who need to abide by the institution's approaches and style. As the late Jack Whittle used to say, "The days of people feeling as though they had to 'genuflect' when they walked into their financial institution are over."

Options Today Force Change

Members have too many options now to tolerate feeling disrespected. Competition from non-credit union competitors has changed financial services forever. Unfortunately for credit unions, many people now think of mortgage companies first.

An Effective Cross-Sales System

Before we even begin this, let me make it clear that you should **NEVER ask your people to push things onto your members that they don't want or need. Without exception.**

That being said, the truth is that most of your members have many wants and needs that remain unmet or that are being taken care of by a competitor. Even if the competitor is doing a good job, the member is STILL not being serviced well because they have to jump through many inconvenient hoops while taking care of several accounts in different places.

The basis of a good cross-sales program is having your people understand the underlying value:

> **"We feel strongly that if we're really taking good care of you, you don't need to go anywhere else to meet any of your financial needs. Period."**

When your people have that much conviction and pride in what you do, they feel comfortable saying this to a potential member or member and MEANING it. Your members will be so attracted to your confidence that they couldn't imagine continuing the old relationships with your competitors. They'll even go through the inconvenience of switching.

With that, you now need to build the cross-sales system on top of it. Using the system without this understanding is like the older women who worked at Kmart stores for years and would, without even making eye contact, smiling, or giving any indication that they were aware of the person at the other end of the receipt, spew out, "Thank you for shopping at Kmart." It just doesn't work.

The Magic of Your Cross-Sales System

Every inquiry should be captured on some form that is constructed to lead a potential member not only into opening an account, but bringing all of their related financial business to you.

The Art and Science of Filling out Forms

There is something magical about forms. When opening a new account, members see that there are questions to be answered and they ready themselves to diligently answer all of them. Unfortunately, the sales staff of most credit unions miss the opportunity completely by asking only contact information questions to open accounts.

When members are open and willing to answer, this is a perfect time to ask really great questions about their other needs and wants, their current financial situation, and possibly what they want to have happen.

What seems to work best is to use a form that not only asks for logistical information, but goes much deeper.

For example, if someone is sitting across the desk wanting to open a certificate of deposit, they are very open to having a few questions asked of them so that they know you are looking out for their best needs.

Example:

1) Before we move ahead, I would like to make sure we're providing you the best possible program that brings you the most value for your situation. I'd like to ask you a few quick questions to make sure we're doing the best thing for you. Would that be okay?

2) Tell me what this CD is for — retirement, a safety net, college, etc.?

3) To make sure we stagger this CD to give you the ease of getting at your money when you need it while **maximizing your return,** tell me what you have in other CDs and savings.

Amount _____ Maturity _____ Rate _____
Where _____

Amount _____ Maturity _____ Rate _____
Where _____

Amount _____ Maturity _____ Rate _____
Where _____

Amount _____ Maturity _____ Rate _____
Where _____

Amount _____ Maturity _____ Rate _____
Where _____

4) How much do you typically keep in savings or a money market? _____ In checking? _____

5) In addition to this, how much do you keep in:

   Money markets _____ Mutual funds _____
   Stocks _____

   IRAs _____ Retirement accounts _____
   Other investments _____ Value of businesses you own _____

6) List the outstanding amounts you have in: Mortgages _____ Credit card debt _____ Car loans _____ Other _____

7) How much and for what are you saving in the areas of:

   Retirement?

   College savings?

   Other?

8) To make sure we serve you best, tell me what you liked about other financial institutions you've worked with and what you didn't like.

9) What services that can make your life easier might you be interested in?

   ___ Overdraft protection ___ Debit card ___ Home equity line with checks ___ Internet bill pay services

With questions similar to these typeset on a form that you require all your new accounts people to fill out and turn in, the amount of your cross-sales will go up astronomically.

Follow Up and Follow Through

If your frontline personnel don't see opportunities, you certainly could have your top sales performers do callbacks after members open their first accounts and talk to them about switching their other accounts. The leveraging of sales talent can give you the best return on investment for that employee or group of employees.

When your staff sees that you are actually . . .

- ✓ compiling and tracking the information they are filling out and
- ✓ creating a callback program for members who have investments and loans elsewhere with solutions to help them more,

they can't help but notice that you're really serious about a solid, successful cross-selling program.

Contrast this to what some credit unions do. Each quarter, they put a new form up in the break room that tracks cross-sales. Sadly, even the credit unions that do this are far ahead of most, who basically do nothing more than talk about cross-sales.

The Four-Step Action Plan to Begin Your Sales Success System

1. **Determine the areas that are most important to systematize.** (For example, rate inquiries for mortgages and deposit accounts might be a good place to start.) I'd recommend that, at the least, you have systems for rate inquiries; managing current accounts; cross-sales of other services; and referrals from realtors, attorneys, CPAs, current members, and others within the credit union.

2. **Create a simple step-by-step system for each area** with **a template form that MUST be filled** out on every inquiry.

3. **Put the necessary tools and materials in place to continuously monitor** that the systems are in place and consistently followed.

4. **Keep adapting, updating, and improving your system.**

Sales Management

Seven Deadly Mistakes Sales Managers Make

1. Seeing the job as administrative.

2. Focusing on low performers.

3. Not celebrating little successes enough.

4. Measuring the wrong things.

5. Not creating systems for rate inquiries, cross-sales, and referral programs.

6. Not creating a system for following up with members after they open accounts.

7. Not monitoring or expecting people to follow the systems.

Correcting the Seven Deadly Mistakes Managers Make

1. Seeing the Job Not as Administrative, But as a Coaching Position

Most sales managers think their job is to review numbers and scold the people who aren't meeting them.

Guilt and shame can motivate over the short term, but the results over the long term are that people's confidence is shaken and they go into a downward spiral. The less confidence they have, the less they feel capable of performing.

In fact, a good sales manager is a coach, a teacher, and an encourager who gets right in there and makes joint calls, sits in on new account openings, and takes every opportunity to make sure salespeople are right on task. Good sales managers will be seen celebrating successes, coaching, and creating improvement plans for employees' weak areas. They develop a rapport with their salespeople, making them want to do better, if for no other reason than to please the sales manager.

Many sales managers have not made the transition to being effective leaders. They spend too much time on their own tasks and transactions with their own members and therefore never capitalize on leveraging themselves by making their people more effective.

2. Focus Not Just on the Low Performers, but on the Top Performers

As with all managers, sales managers fall into the trap of giving their attention to the low performers while virtually ignoring the top performers.

When I was first introduced to the concept of under-performers actually under-performing so they would receive more attention, I thought it was ludicrous. These are adults, and that is very childish behavior. However, after seeing it happen over and over again, I now believe that people will in fact, do whatever it takes to get attention. Whether it's done consciously or subconsciously, it happens.

Rationale for Spending More Time on Top Performers

If, however, you have a top performer who is doing $4 million in new business in a month and a low performer who is doing $300,000, by simply coaching the top performer to increase production by 10 percent, you have a far better chance of increasing your gross sales than you would by asking the low performer to double production.

Since we tend to get what we reward, spending too much time with low performers tends to support those who have the least potential to increase your results. Of course, this doesn't mean you should ignore them and not help them, as there are many who can be helped substantially when the light goes on. The point is to be in constant contact with and to lavish appreciation on those who do perform.

3. Celebrate Little and Big Successes Constantly

The one element that is by far the most consistent among the top-performing credit unions we interviewed is that of celebration. Celebration for them is scheduled, it's powerful, and it's fun.

Most top-performing credit unions schedule at least a full evening once per quarter to celebrate and train their staff. It is a high-energy event with lots of encouragement and celebration. There is no focus on what isn't working. That can best be handled at smaller meetings. The big rallies are only celebratory.

In addition, I've seen all kinds of fun things credit unions do to celebrate moment by moment. One credit union has a horn that is blown when a new member signs up with them. One CEO, with a lot of voice lessons under his belt, actually sings to his employees before opening every morning about what he wants them to do. Many management teams put on skits introducing a new concept or how they want members handled. The skits include crazy costuming, music, and all kinds of theatrical displays to make it fun.

4. Measure the Right Things

What to measure? As the old adage goes,

> **"What gets measured . . . gets done."**

Unfortunately, most credit union sales managers measure ONLY the results, assuming this will compel their people to get to those results. Most people have a difficult time understanding how their behaviors create the results.

High-performing financial organizations measure the behaviors that get them to where they need to be. Some behaviors we've seen credit unions measure include:

- ✓ Number of loan applications taken
- ✓ Number of sales calls
- ✓ Number of referrals to other departments
- ✓ Number of referrals from members asking directly for that officer
- ✓ Retention of members
- ✓ Number of services sold per member meeting

You want to measure these behaviors by team and by individual. Then you can celebrate and create hoopla over the numbers and how they are increasing to keep the focus clearly on the right things.

5. Create a System for Tracking Rate Inquiries, Cross-Sales and Referral Programs

Intentions are good. Training is great. But the only thing that will give sustainable and dramatic results is having systems in place and MONITORING all of them. Period.

6. Create a System for Following Up with Members After They Open Accounts

Credit union members are notoriously underserved and treated with indifference. After they open an account, they probably will never again receive personal correspondence from their credit union. Often the only news they get is in the form of a statement or an overdraft notice — not exactly a bonding experience.

- ✓ Create a system where each new account receives a personalized handwritten thank-you within 24 hours.

- ✓ Send another letter a week later.

- ✓ Follow up with a call one month later.

- ✓ From that point on, create a system whereby each member is grouped with others of common interest and they receive occasional tips or articles that may be helpful for them.

Notice I'm not talking about sending some glossy brochure that is not personalized.

Make sure you track retention and create systems to hang onto the business you worked hard for.

7. Expect and Require Your People to Follow the Systems

If you can't get your people to follow your systems, you probably can't get your kids to come home by curfew. It's about people not really believing your expectations. Look at the ways people slide by and you will notice that the old "give an inch and they take a mile" syndrome quickly destroys your ability to get results.

Ask for compliance often in a systemized way. If you don't get what you ask for, immediately confront the guilty party. If you still don't get it, make sure there are consequences.

Even if one of your top performers won't do it, you must deal with them. Jack Welch has said, "If you have a top performer who doesn't share your values, they still need to go."

Sales culture is still a myth in most credit unions. It receives a lot of lip service, but there isn't much walk behind the talk.

- ✓ Take the time to create systems.
- ✓ Monitor them.
- ✓ Reward them.

When you do all this, then you will have the groundwork for a solid sales culture that creates sustainable and exciting results!

Summary

Just as it is said, "Without advertising, there are no sales," so it is said, "Without sales, there is no business." This can also be said in a more positive way: "Great advertising sparks sales, and sales are the beginning, not the end, of success."

By doing a few simple things you can break through the "order-taking" habit forever and profit many times over as a result. Teach your personnel to go beyond order-taking and ask questions that are key to finding out how you can serve members better and get all of their financially related business. Give help wherever possible. Build confidence in your potential members and members so that they feel you are their safety net. You are there to help them make the right decisions for their financial security and well-being. Above all, make sure your staff is motivated to make a difference for members. If so, the growth will come.

Action Plan for Implementing Strategies in Chapter 6

Action to Take	Responsible Person	Results	Start Date	Target Date

Benefits

7 Breakthrough to Extraordinary High-Performance People

Creating and Building a Staff of Top Performers

Many credit unions are under the mistaken belief that their assets are listed on their balance sheet. Smart credit unions know their most important asset is their staff of well-hired, well-trained, passionate, and committed people. It's much easier to attract and keep high-quality employees when they feel part of something extraordinary.

Yet, most credit unions themselves are well trained and wonderfully skilled only at the technical parts of their work. It's as if the same brain that allows someone to grow and manage a high-quality loan portfolio has restricted blood flow to the part which allows that person to be a genius at motivating and exciting employees to work smarter and create better results.

What are the philosophies that guide the top-performing leaders to attain great results from their people?

Values-Driven Organizations

Values drive the results of the successful organization. Top-performing members of your staff who don't share your values have got to go. They will intoxicate the culture and diffuse all of your leadership efforts.

What Are the Core Values of Top-Performing Organizations?

Value Number 1
"No Excuses" Leadership

When interviewing the sales manager of one of the largest and most successful mortgage lending departments in the country, I asked her what was the biggest difference between the high performers and the low performers. Without hesitation, she said, "Excuses."

She explained, "My top people never have excuses. The lower half are always blaming underwriting, the latest merger, the new software system, and on and on. My top performers have been through all the same things. They just keep on going without excuses."

When you remove people's ability to live in their "excuse" zone, there is no place for them to go but up — or out.

Not allowing excuses is really a matter of integrity and truth. Unfortunately, it's really not very common. In his book, *The Day America Told the Truth*, James Patterson says that when Americans were asked if they lie regularly, 91 percent responded yes.

Numerous studies have proven that integrity is the number one attribute that people feel makes a leader powerful. Leaders, we must remember, include not only those who hold positions of power but also those who have the personal power to persuade others.

Most individuals, when asked if they live their lives with integrity, would agree that they do. Yet there are hundreds of ways in which people, including those considered leaders, fail to keep their word every day. They allow their own excuses and the excuses of others to undermine their power.

Most of these are considered standard business fare and are rarely brought to light as exceptions to honesty. Here are some examples that rob us of our personal leadership power:

- A manager sets a standard of performance that she expects her staff to meet. When they don't, she chooses to avoid conflict and doesn't confront the situation. By not addressing it, she basically has said that what she declared as important is not that important. Those who ask for a sales culture but don't create systems and monitor them basically have sent the message that it's lip service. They are not credible. Other expectations that they set will not be regarded as important either. It sends things into a downward spiral that is hard to stop.

- A manager calls an 8 a.m. meeting after consulting everyone involved about the best meeting time. Several people come late. These people have not lived up to their word because they were not there when they said they would be. They have shown a lack of integrity.

- Jane, the loan processor, said she would have the project concluded by Friday. On Friday, the end is nowhere in sight.

This sounds too harsh, you say. Jane didn't lie. She was held up by others and just got behind. That may be true, *but* she had a commitment. A commitment that she did not meet. Missed deadlines, late arrivals at meetings, and failures to confront unacceptable work are common because we can find a seemingly legitimate excuse for every exception to the rule. The amazing thing about excuses is that they sound so good — so justifiable. Sometimes they even attract empathy. However legitimate or convincing it sounds, an excuse is an excuse and a story is a story.

There is hardly a human alive who, when reading this, isn't feeling his or her ears get a little hot. It is part of the human condition to fail, but strong leaders rarely have excuses for not following through while weaker leaders tend to consider it "normal" and have their own set of excuses to legitimatize their failures to live up to their commitments.

If you are one of those leaders who need help in this area, tell your people the truth and tell them it is a weakness you want to improve. Ask them to help you by coaching you, and create systems that make improvement necessary.

By being honest, others will do whatever they can to help keep you on task. They know this will help them also, because they are more effective when you, as their leader, are rigorous about your commitments.

People who are leaders, whether by virtue of a position they hold or simply because of the personal power they possess, commit themselves to integrity.

> In the Dr. Seuss book, *Horton Hatches an Egg*, Horton (the elephant) is asked by Mayzie (the bird who laid the egg) to lie on her egg until she returns from a short trip. Mayzie gets wrapped up with enjoying her freedom and chooses not to return. Horton is left to sit on the egg. Through ice storms, safari hunts, and an unwelcome trip to the zoo, Horton perseveres. As he meets each

challenge that rubs against his commitment, he repeats, "I said what I meant and I meant what I said, an elephant is faithful, 100 percent."

Horton understood the power of commitment and decided that he should live by his word — in spite of the fact that the rules had changed, in spite of the exceptions, in spite of the stories, and in spite of the fact that others let him down.

If there ever was an elephant that was a leader, it was Horton. He did what he said he would do. His actions were consistent with his words. Most importantly, he managed to live by his word when excuses were abundant.

Immediate Excuse Awareness

One of the first places I always start when trying to create better results for an organization is with the concept of immediate awareness of excuses. I help not only the leadership team but also everyone in the credit union by asking them to publicly display their awareness whenever a colleague begins to use an excuse. When confronted with an excuse or a story of why something didn't happen or couldn't happen, I ask them to stick their fingers in their ears and repeat,

"I'm not listening, I'm not listening."

When people realize their excuses no longer hold any credibility, the excuses suddenly lose all their energy and eventually go away. People then focus their energy on results as opposed to perfecting their "stories" of why things couldn't be done.

When human error happens, a simple "I'm sorry" or "I'm sorry, I'm working on getting better on this and would appreciate your help" is a wonderfully grown-up approach as opposed to spewing out the "story."

Wouldn't it be nice if you could count on Hortons in your workplace? Better yet, wouldn't it be great if you could live like Horton? Your colleagues need you to be Horton-like. If I were the egg, I'd hang with Horton. He's my leader.

Value Number 2
Hitting Conflict Head-on

Conflict is part of life. Always has been. Always will be. And yet conflict kills many organizations while strengthening others. How is this true?

In Jim Collins' book *Good to Great*, he tells about a study of companies that had done well for years and then shifted to greatness and sustained it. One of the most significant findings he discusses in his book was that the leadership staff duked it out in the most grown-up of ways. If they disagreed, they fought with all their energy for their ideas.

Instead of attacking people, which is prevalent in low-performing organizations, they attacked ideas with complete respect for each other as humans. When they walked out of the meeting room, they fully understood each other. They left the meeting with a uniform and powerful plan. No undermining or dysfunctional complaining behind the scenes occurred.

> I worked with a large organization that employed a man (I'll call him Ron) who had only two years left until

retirement. Before starting a major turnaround initiative, I asked the CEO what was the biggest hurdle he had in leading that financial institution. He said it was Ron. He said no matter what he did to get the troops to rally in the same direction, Ron would leave the senior management meeting and whine to his staff about how stupid the CEO and the rest of the senior management team were. Of course, the staff was demoralized.

He felt trapped by Ron. "We can't fire him. He only has two years until retirement," the president said.

I told him that all of the systems and staff training that normally create miraculous results wouldn't work without Ron on board emotionally. The training would only frustrate the staff even more in the presence of such a "negative cheerleader." He would rob them of all their energy and reinforce reasons why nothing proposed would work, leaving them thinking, "Why bother to follow such a dumb system?"

Since every problem in an organization is ALWAYS a leadership issue, I always start by meeting with the leadership team first. I knew that the primary objective of this meeting was to help Ron make a shift — either emotionally or by physically making a move to a different employer on a voluntary basis.

About 30 minutes into the session, I asked the group if it might be helpful to know what the biggest hurdle was that they would need to overcome. Of course they were excited to know so they wouldn't have to revisit the school of hard knocks.

I replied, "Every organization has its 'whiners.' They are the energy suckers. They make people feel bad about themselves. They make people feel insecure and uncomfortable that maybe they're whining about them too, behind their backs. They're no fun to work with. They won't be honest up-front and fight for what they believe, but they'll walk out of a meeting and go on a crusade to let everyone know that the leaders are stupid. I suspect you have them here, and I'll bet you even know who they are. And you're probably under the mistaken belief that it would be difficult to fire them.

"The reality is, they are not only hurting the organization, they are probably causing dysfunction, even depression, for the employees who must work around them. They MUST change. You owe it to the people around them and to your organization.

"You must confront them and lovingly give them two choices. Choice number one is that they change immediately. Choice number two is that they find employment that makes them happy, and if it isn't here, they should find that place soon, for their own good."

I reinforced this fact as I said, "The whiners need to be confronted and asked to change their behavior. Let them know that it's important to you that they bring all their skills, their passion, and their energy to work each day and go home feeling thrilled about what they did that day. Let them know that you have noticed they're not happy and that it is not acceptable for anyone to live that way. Let them know you want them to tell you in the next 24 hours if they think they can come along with the team and bring their spirit or if they'd like to begin to look for another place of employment that would better fulfill their needs. Life is too short to be miserable.

"Most organizations are under the mistaken belief that they can't terminate people who are near retirement or in protected classes — or whatever. The reality is that most states have 'employment at will' clauses and the lawsuits that result are usually from more barbaric approaches to 'firing' people.

"An invitation to these people to decide what they want and providing them with a way to save face by giving them time to look for a job while they are still employed is a wonderfully compassionate way to let them move on or commit to something different."

Out of the corner of my eye, I watched Ron swallow and slouch down in his chair.

I followed up that conversation with, "It's your job in leadership to coach those people to rise to the occasion or invite them to find work that makes them happy." Then I went on to other topics as if I knew nothing about the primary culprit being right there in the room.

Before the end of the meeting, I explained that in a few hours I would be asking their employees to make some substantial shifts in how they perform. I added that employees would be watching to see if the management team was willing to make changes too. Therefore, the changes that management made needed to be profound and easily observable to ensure the best results for their direct reports.

I asked the management team to individually share their commitments of what they would do differently to create an extraordinary result.

One by one each committed to change. When it came to Ron's turn, he looked around the room and did one of the bravest things I've ever seen. He said, "I think I'm that whiner, and I see how I've hurt this place and the people in it. My commitment to all of you is that I will stop. If you see me do it again, you have my permission to be a huge and immediate interruption."

I'm always amazed at the conflicts that go on for years in organizations, building in intensity and draining those involved of their energy.

It shouldn't be that shocking to me, since I came from a home where conflict was swept under the rug. It was my mother's belief that a home just shouldn't have any of THAT. So, if one person would confront another about some inappropriate behavior, she would make a gesture of peace and say something along the lines of, "Let's just all be happy."

Of course, we don't know what we don't know until we see ourselves through another's eyes. When my sister brought home a boyfriend from college, he kept remarking over and over again, "I don't get it. Nobody's fighting. Your family is really boring."

Now I would agree that the lack of yelling and calling of names was probably a good thing for our family. However, there were many unresolved issues that built tensions. If these had been dealt with immediately they could have created a more harmonious effect, deeper relationships, and trust.

Unfortunately, we learn most of our conflict-resolution skills in the fourth grade on the playground. If we have a problem with Joe, we go directly to Sue and tell her that Joe's a jerk!

Not only does that not help Joe get any better, it causes Sue to feel she can't trust us to be honest with her. And Joe, on some level, feels the tension and has no tools to break through.

When we have conflict, we just need to hit it head-on. However, instead of attacking the person head-on we should tell that person what we need more and less of.

Examples:

> "I need to count on the fact that when you say you'll get me a report by Tuesday, even if the place is burned down, you'll find me, report in hand."

> "When you walk into meetings late, it sends a message to our staff that their time is not valuable or the topic of the meeting isn't valuable. I need you to be in the meeting room two minutes before the meeting starts."

The reality is that when you come from a place of love instead of anger, you can tell anybody anything. If you come from a place of retaliation (I'll hurt you back because you hurt me), you can be assured that they will not be open to your ideas, and they'll be putting up a powerful defense.

> One of the most difficult conflicts I have had to confront was with an exchange student who was to live with us for a year. In the first week of his stay, his English was very weak, and I knew only two words in his language. I had heard them used when my father hit his finger with a

hammer! It was clear those words wouldn't be of much help on this.

So communication was difficult. As the situation became more uncomfortable, I became more anxious. The problem was that he had terrible body odor, which got worse each day. The country he came from is known for weekly bathing. Also, I suspected the number of people there with bad teeth was indicative that many areas of hygiene weren't perceived as important.

In the pattern I learned from my mother, I chose to ignore it for many days. One evening, he had offered to help make dinner and learn how to cook American food. I was thrilled — until I realized how small the kitchen suddenly felt as the odor brought me to the point of feeling ill. I was wondering how I'd ever be able to eat!

My first thought was, "Somebody's got to talk to this kid." Of course no one else was going to, except perhaps a fellow student at the high school who would probably deliver it in a package that ripped at his self-esteem for years.

After minutes of jittery small talk, preparing myself for the big "hit," I finally said, "Say, I've been noticing that there is an unusual smell. I'm not sure, but I think it is a body odor . . .." At this point, I was stumbling over my words. "And, I'm wondering if, if, well, if you took a shower today?"

He looked at me as if he was confused by the English. "Yes, I took a shower."

Oh great, I thought. Now what do I do? And then it hit me. "Well, how about your clothes? Are all of your clothes fresh today?"

"Oh, no. I've been wearing this shirt for four days," he replied.

Aha! That was it. "Oh, I see. Well, I'd like to suggest you try something different while in America. Americans usually shower every day and put on clean clothes every day. After wearing your clothes, put them in that basket in your room. In a few days, they magically show up, clean and folded in your drawer."

He smiled.

After dinner, he helped clean the kitchen. He looked up from placing dishes in the dishwasher and said, "I appreciate your helping me. Students notice when I'm different. I want to be like an American while in America. Thank you for telling me."

Whew.

It became clear to me on that day:

> **When you come from a place of caring and love, you can tell anyone just about anything.**

Although I would like to believe that adults are all capable of working through conflict in an adult way, I find that most struggle. A leader in an organization needs to make sure that he or she creates a climate where conflict is hit head-on. That way, the ugly festering of unresolved issues doesn't get in the way of the organization's performance.

Value Number 3
Playful Celebration

One of the most profound things that stood out in our interviews of top-performing credit unions was that their leaders had consistently scheduled and structured celebrations of success. Even during bad times, they still celebrated what was going well. They always found something to celebrate.

Perhaps this has to do with energy. When we feel as if we're losing, there is an energy drain that causes us to believe we're losers. When we take time to celebrate our success, we can't help but feel a little better about ourselves.

> In my office during our weekly staff meetings, one of our most successful practices is to start with five minutes of "positive focus." We go around the room, and each person must speak about what he or she accomplished that week and what miracles he or she saw others perform.
>
> Just last week, I felt as though it was one of my least productive weeks and my results were not high. When we started the positive focus, suddenly a list of very significant accomplishments came spewing out of my mouth. Also, my staff reminded me of several accomplishments I had missed. I suddenly felt reenergized and renewed. Then I remembered how important it is to focus on the positive things and

constantly build self-esteem of the entire staff on a regular basis.

The CEO of a very high-growth, high-performing financial organization, does a "birthday breakfast" once a month during which he, as president, meets with his employees who have birthdays that month. No officers are allowed. They chat about what works and what employees need in order to work better. He also has quarterly staff meetings that focus on sales and service training and celebration of what happened that quarter.

In fact, I can't think of one top-performing credit union that doesn't do a quarterly meeting with a focus on celebration and a fun approach to training. In addition to scheduled events, some credit unions have fun celebrations based on short-term results.

However you skin the cat, you can't ignore the correlation between a sense of play and celebration and results within the industry. Outside the industry, you need not look any further than the top-performing stock of the last 30 years, Southwest Airlines, to see how a sense of play and celebration can strengthen and unify an organization.

Value Number 4
Sense of Urgency

Rome wasn't built in a day, but I'll bet it would have been built a little more quickly had there been more sense of urgency.

Things take as much time as you give them. The "conventional wisdom" says that building a sales culture takes between two and five years. To that I say, "Only if you say so." I've seen it done with great success in less than two months.

Many times, when working with a management team, I'll give them an exercise to do and set it up like this:

> "Now, I know many of you have done something like this before and you know it takes about three hours. Since things take as much time as you give them, I'll give you five minutes and what you'll produce will be extraordinary. Begin."

There is a flurry of activity for five minutes. Sure enough, at the end of that time, they have done masterful work. Had they taken the additional two hours and 55 minutes, they probably wouldn't have done as well.

A sense of urgency is necessary in any corporate change. Without proclaiming that urgency, most initiatives hit roadblocks, to which the reaction is typically, "Oops, hit a roadblock. I guess we can't go any further."

When the sense of urgency is there, suddenly people realize they'll just have to figure out how to get around that roadblock right now! And remarkably, they do.

During a kickoff program, we create a tremendous amount of excitement and enthusiasm during the program. When people feel they can be much better than they are, most tend to be quite thrilled at the prospect of feeling more competent.

After the kickoff session, the systems introduced have to be implemented immediately. I tell the management team prior to a session that they MUST create an immediate sense of urgency to implement the systems discussed in the session. I usually suggest they start a Mystery Shopping program at 8 a.m. the next day. They must let their people know that starting the next morning, they WILL be shopped to make sure they are immediately implementing the new systems.

With a sense of urgency among employees that they must implement the new systems immediately, guess what happens?

They implement them immediately!

Several credit unions have tried to save a few bucks by not doing the Mystery Shopping. Although they tend to get fairly good results, these results are not even a fraction as dramatic or sustainable as those credit unions that have a good Mystery Shopping program.

The chief operating officer of my company, who does the hiring for us, mentioned that she likes to take a drive somewhere with a job candidate because she gets a feel for the person's sense of urgency about life. People who drive with a sense of urgency, not recklessly but with a focus toward results, tend to live their entire lives with a sense of urgency.

Laid-back people are wonderful, but they rarely become high performers and deliver great service. You need people who want to shake it up and make great things happen quickly after an idea strikes. Then they will always be ready to implement the next great idea.

Value Number 5
Deeper-level Truth Telling

The deeper level of truth telling about which I am talking is best illustrated by an experience I had several years ago.

> I was only 19 when I interned for the summer as a 4-H agent. For you city slickers who don't know what that means, it's an organization that helps country kids develop leadership skills by teaching them how to take pride in developing projects. My job was to be in charge of speaking to the area 4-H clubs and managing the small animals at the county fair. Incidentally, all went well, with the exception of the bunny that escaped from her cage and was accidentally stepped on by a horse . . . (one of those days you don't soon forget).
>
> The biggest lesson I learned that summer was after the fair ended and the county agent in charge of the office came to me and said, "Roxanne, now I'm going to teach you about budgeting. What you need to do is see what you spent this year as compared to last year. Then tack on some more so we can go to the county board and ask for more than we really need."
>
> "More than we need," I said in my naïve innocence. "Why would we do something like that? Besides, I spent less money than we spent last year so we could actually decrease the budget."
>
> "Oh my," the agent said. "Let's see. How can I explain this? Okay, it goes like this. When you ask the county board for money, no matter how much you ask for,

you're going to get less. So you have to ask for more, and then when they do cut you back, you can yell and scream and wave your arms, so they'll increase it. The game goes back and forth a few times, and eventually you want to end up with a little more than what you had last year."

"Hmmm…I see. So it's basically a game where nobody tells the truth?" I asked.

"Yes, that's it!" he said.

"Well, I've got a great idea," I said. "Why don't we go to the county board this year and tell them that THIS year, we're going to tell them the truth and we want them to do that as well?"

I thought the poor man was going to lose bladder control. He found that to be quite humorous. I, on the other hand, was quite sincere.

Yes, I found out that summer one important fact of business life:

> **Budgeting is only one of the multitudes of accepted ways of doing business that elicit "structured distrust."**

When you're lying and everyone knows you're lying, does that make it okay?

Another way that credit union management teams repeatedly display a lack of deeper truth telling is when they walk out of meetings and share their disagreement about the decisions with the rest of the team. Then they follow it with, "I told you so."

One phenomenon I consistently notice in the top-performing organizations is that the game playing, the passive-aggressive behaviors, the sabotaging, and the backhanded comments are almost nonexistent. During management meetings, the bottom line is that people openly disagree with each other and it's absolutely safe to do so without repercussion. The truth is not held back. The management team leaves each meeting feeling like they were heard, even if they didn't get their way.

Value Number 6
High Expectations

There has been a lot of research done on firstborn children. It seems that over 88 percent of graduate students, 68 percent of presidents, 80 percent of entrepreneurs, and 23 of the first 24 astronauts just so happen to be firstborn children.

So what is the conditioning we give to our firstborn children that the later siblings don't seem to receive?

1) Reinforcement. We tend to take a plethora of pictures of firstborn children compared to their siblings. By the time that last child comes along, the film budget seems to have dwindled to practically nothing. My youngest sister has only one portrait from her childhood. If that wouldn't send you to therapy, what would?

2) Expectations. No matter how old the oldest is, he or she always seems to get to be in charge of the younger siblings. A six-year-old is in charge of his four-year-old sister. But when the sister is six, her eight-year-old brother is STILL in charge.

People rise to the level of the expectations put on them.

> I remember I once asked an intern in my office to mock up a mailing piece that was to be sent to CEOs and association executive directors. She put together a piece that looked more like a flyer you'd hang on the church bulletin board than something that would be well received by executives.
>
> Interns can be rather fragile, as they're just learning, and their successes come hard early in a career. I knew I needed to handle the situation with tenderness, but I also knew that she was capable of more.
>
> As delicately as I could, I looked at her and said, "Gosh, I think you have more in you. What I want you to do is pretend like you've been doing this forever, and you've just received an award for the work you've done in matching your message and presentation to the audience. Go back and spend another hour on this like your life depended on creating the best possible mailing piece to catch a CEO's attention."
>
> She came back an hour later with a piece that made everyone in the office gasp with delight. What a shocking difference! She immediately asked if she could have a copy for her portfolio and turn it in for her internship grade. She had found a new level of pride.

When we take the time to coach people to a level of performance beyond what they thought was possible, magnificent things happen to their performance and their belief in their capabilities.

Identify your values carefully, evangelize them, and live them incessantly. Your values are the foundation upon which your credit union is built. Make it strong.

Start with the Right People

Last night, I told a complete stranger who was checking me out at a store that I was writing a book on better financial services. She went crazy and held my purchase for 10 minutes. She told me of the problems she has had with simple transactions at her bank and that she now was in the process of withdrawing her money. "After a string of about 15 errors, I went to the manager who told me, 'Hey, I am sorry. We just cannot find good people.'"

Financial institutions today are beset with high rates of turnover, underperformance, salespeople with no aptitude for sales, employee litigation, wrongful hiring claims, employee theft — and the list goes on. These risks are increased exponentially when you hire the wrong person.

The wrong person is under-qualified, lacking in adequate emotional intelligence, misplaced, and litigious. This can cause great disruption and loss of growth and morale for the entire organization.

In the following section, we'll look intently at the hiring process to discover what works and what doesn't work when attempting to find and keep the right people.

Recruiting, Interviewing, Hiring, and Training Great Employees!

Part A: Recruiting Great Employees

Define the Position.

Before you even begin your recruiting efforts for a new position, you first need to clearly define your expectations for the position. The following are four easy steps to help you do so:

1. Make a list of the top five things a person MUST do to be successful in this job. These performance objectives are the foundation of your search.

2. Take each task and apply the standard goal-setting parameter of SMART: **S**pecific, **M**easurable, **A**ction oriented, **R**esult defined, and **T**ime based.

3. Focus on major objectives and the steps necessary to achieve those objectives. Examples could be technical objectives, team objectives, problems that must be solved, or changes that need to be made.

4. Create a new job description that lists all of the tasks and goals you expect the person to achieve, not what qualifications you expect the person to have. Note: Just because someone meets your statistical qualifications (e.g., by possessing a certain degree or years of experience), that doesn't mean they'll do a good job.

Examples:

Performance Profile: Marketing Director

Wrong: B.S. degree in marketing.

Right: **Prepare time-phased competitive analysis in three market areas. Complete within three months.**

Wrong: 3-5 years industry experience.

Right: **Evaluate impact of marketing plan and positioning statement. Complete by March.**

Wrong: Good planning skills.

Right: **Develop a marketing plan and calendar of promotions. Complete by July.**

Wrong: Good interpersonal skills.

Right: **Collaborate with sales manager to develop product positioning, pricing, and marketing campaign for November launch.**

Wrong: Ability to make board presentations.

Right: **Gather input from all functions and present plan deviations, changes, compliances, and results to board each month.**

Wrong: Ability to think creatively and strategically at product and market level.

Right: **By September, develop three-year product plan with feature, revenue, and market share analysis based on various pricing and margin estimates.**

Power Recruiting

Now that you know exactly the type of employee you're after, it's time to start looking. Unfortunately, the best employees are usually those who are already employed. So if you want to add them to your team, you'll have to create ads that are compelling enough to lure them away from their current employers.

The following are five easy ways to write such an ad:

1. Spell out EXPECTED ACCOMPLISHMENTS

Gear half of your recruitment ad toward what you expect the employee to accomplish. This will attract the overachievers and discourage those who like to talk about work but don't necessarily get it done with great results.

Examples:

> "Lead our sales team of 50 to a number one market share!"

> "Create meaningful member relationships that earn/attract all of their financial business."

2. Spell out THE FUTURE

Create a vivid picture of the growth and learning opportunities your credit union offers. This will attract employees who are committed to building a great career and future with you.

Examples:

> "Become an Internet marketing guru as you execute a state-of-the-art marketing process on the Internet."

> "Develop your leadership skills as you open our new location in Charlotte."

3. Omit DETAILS

Resist including a laundry list of requirements, duties, educational requirements, or skills in your ad. This can scare off even the best of candidates. Experience is also a poor indicator of future success, so spend no more than one sentence on these types of details. Keep them vague and simple.

Example:

> "Industry experience and a track record of success in operations are helpful."

4. Lead with a GRIPPING TITLE

Make your ad titles as creative and interesting as possible. Remember, you're competing against hundreds of mundane ads for attention. A unique and captivating title will do just the trick.

Examples:

> Instead of "Internet Developer Wanted," say, **"Seeking Internet Sales Guru"**

> Instead of "Sales Management Officer Wanted,"

say, **"Can You Lead Others to Be Sales Wizards?"**

5. Quickly DISQUALIFY

The end of your ad should ask candidates to submit a few paragraphs describing their most significant related accomplishment. This goes far beyond their resume in helping you identify their history of success and compatibility with your job opening.

Bad Ad Example:

Call Center Manager

The Call Center Manager is responsible for managing a team of 25 telephone salespeople in our Dakota market. At least five years of experience in the area of financial institution sales, plus at least three years of supervisory experience, is necessary. B.S. degree is required. Compensation package is comparable to industry standards.

Good Ad Example:

Seeking High-Impact, Hands-On Sales Manager to Bring Us to Number 1 in the Market

Our credit union will soon be implementing an exciting new method of helping members meet their financial goals. If you can hire, train, and develop a team of high-performing internal salespeople, you'll have the time of your life! We've dedicated first-priority resources to this expansion. So if you want an opportunity to build something great, send your resume with an example of your best sales leadership accomplishment to . . .

Best Places to Place Ads:

- Word of Mouth
- Direct Sourcing
- Internet
- Employment Agencies
- Advertising
- Job Fairs
- Professional Associations

Six Essential Steps to an Effective Recruiting Ad

- Powerful title: Use interesting and exciting titles for your positions!

- Marketing description: Market to them. Don't sell.

- List performance objectives: High-performing people are motivated by what they will be learning, doing, and becoming.

- Include skills: Describe only the minimal amount of years and skills needed, as broader availability will pull a larger group of candidates.

- Define the growth opportunity: Job candidates want to see opportunities for growth and what they look like.

- Add contact information: Encourage the candidate to do more than send a resume. Lead them to review your Web site. They should walk into an interview fully understanding your business and what you're about.

Part B: Interviewing

According to a Michigan State University study, the typical employment interview is only 57 percent accurate as a predictor of future performance. **The study found that too much interviewing emphasis is put on evaluating skills and personality. Instead, the focus should be on past performance.**

An effective interview can uncover the common characteristics of most top performers. What you ultimately want to determine is if they have:

- A track record of high energy and team leadership;

- A demonstrated record of comparable past performance; and

- A strong ability to adapt and produce in a new environment.

Powerful Interview Questions

Focus your interview on determining the candidate's history of results — not on personality or skills. It's easy to get lured into wanting to hire a great personality. However, ultimately you need the job done and you want people who are **capable of seeing what isn't there and making it happen.** You want a team of people who consistently get superior results.

Here are a few questions to help you sniff out a person's capacity to consistently deliver results:

1. What's been your most significant accomplishment in each of your past two or three jobs?

2. For each of your past two or three jobs, tell me about your most significant team or management achievement.

3. One of our key objectives for the person who is offered this position will be to _____ (describe a top performance objective). Can you tell me about your most important comparable accomplishments?

4. If you were offered this position, how would you go about implementing _____? (Describe top two or three performance objectives your organization has established for the position.)

5. If I were meeting you here three years from today, what must happen, both personally and professionally, for you to feel good about your accomplishments in this position? (Note that if they can't answer this question or their answers are flaky, they probably have limited abilities to be results focused.)

6. If I were to hire you, why would I later feel like you provided one of the best returns on any investment I've ever made in an employee?

Psychological Testing

One of the best ways to decrease your chances of a bad hire is to do psychological testing. In my own business, I find that all the caution indicators on a future employee's psychological testing results turn out to accurately predict eventual challenges with the employee.

An increasing number of companies are using psychological testing to improve the consistency of accurate hiring decisions. The American Management Association reported that 44 percent of its responding members used testing for hiring decisions.

After having reviewed hundreds of different employment tests, the one I find to be extremely effective and predictive also is used by a Fortune 500 automotive company, whose representative said:

> "Historically, our industry experiences extremely high turnover, and as such we have been looking for a tool to help put the right person in the right job. Since we began using a psychologically based selection tool to help in our sales selection process, our retention has jumped from 10 to 77 percent, which we have calculated saved us $32 million over the past twelve months in related turnover and lost opportunity costs." (Regina Roat, human resources director, Sterling McCall Toyota, Houston, Texas)

If 40 percent of the Fortune 100 companies use some form of psychological testing for pre-employment screening, there must be some evidence it works; otherwise they wouldn't spend the money.

Finding high-performance salespeople who fit into a particular culture is at the top of most executives' minds today. It seems like finding someone who fits both performance-goal criteria and social objectives is nearly impossible.

What you want is to evaluate the true potential and level of risk associated with the people you interview by using an **objective behavioral assessment to identify behavior critical to success.**

It's not prudent and is on the verge of fiscal mismanagement to consider hiring a lender, a business development officer, or a teller who isn't tested. And you absolutely can't afford to hire an executive who doesn't test well. The cultural damage that can be done in the few months it takes to get rid of a bad hire can eat into your growth for years.

Today, several excellent sources do psychological testing over the Internet very inexpensively. The testing and can be done in 15 minutes, and the results can be sent via e-mail immediately.

We are constantly reviewing testing instruments. For a list of our current recommendations, visit www.EmmerichFinancial.com.

Background Check

Did you know that 33% of job applicants falsify their employment applications? Are you aware that 3.2 million workplace crimes happen each year? A staggering 20 percent of people in today's workforce have a CRIMINAL record. So how do you protect yourself from the growing numbers of untruthful and unlawful violations in the workplace?

Many companies are afraid of engaging in extensive background investigations. They're concerned about compliance with EEOC and legislative privacy mandates. Don't be. Potential problems can be avoided by securing releases from job candidates and/or their previous employers that exempt you from any liability associated with such investigations. Have each candidate fill out a release form that allows you to do a search.

One inexpensive resource to do a trace on Social Security information, verify identity and countries of residence, do a criminal record and motor vehicle search, and obtain education verification is found online at www.HireRight.com. It is a very worthwhile investment.

Part C: Hiring

Good hiring is best accomplished by asking the right questions and appraising the answers objectively. Most interview questions don't get to the core of what you need to know.

Objectively Assessing the Candidate

<u>Sample questions you need to answer:</u>

Can the person do the job?
- What successes has this person had that are transferable?
- Where has this person under performed?
- Has the person's education and work been relevant and sufficient to equip her for this job?
- In what ways will the person's skills and experiences enable him to do the job and allow him to advance?
- Does she have the stamina necessary for the job?
- How competent and productive has this person been?

Will the person do the job?
- What motivates this person?
- If this person has what it takes to do the job, is he motivated to do an extraordinary job?
- Does she have the drive to function near full potential?
- Is this person willing to go above and beyond what is necessary?
- To what extent will this person take the initiative in getting a task done on time?

How does this person relate with other people?

- How compatible is this person with the job and your organization's culture?
- How will others get along with this person?
- How does this person deal with roadblocks and other frustrations?
- What beliefs guide this person?
- How would this person impact co-workers?
- After the interview, did you feel invigorated or drained from this person's energy?

Making the Offer

Top-performing organizations tend to pay their employees far more than their competitors. They want to hire the best; therefore, they know they need to pay well. High pay for average performance, however, is a path to disaster.

Before making your offer, research the salary for the position and your location.

The Internet can be extremely helpful. *The Wall Street Journal Online* gives information like:

> *The **Chief Credit Executive** working in **MN - Statewide** now earns an average salary of **$63,360**. Half of those in this position would earn between **$40,265** and **$73,953** (the 17th and 67th percentiles). These numbers are derived from real, area specific, survey data.*
>
> *When benefits and bonuses are added to this salary, the average total compensation for this position would be **$79,471**. The report*

below also explains how the cost-of-living in this location affects the actual value of this salary.

The offer is a sales process:
- Determine what a potential employee wants out of the position. For many people, salary is not as important as other components of the job. Find out what they want.
- Find out about any objections that they may not have disclosed. Know exactly what you are pitching and what the hurdles are so you can put together an action plan that exactly addresses these things.

After the Offer

The period after the offer is often a time when people begin to experience buyer's remorse. Did they really make a good decision in accepting the job?

Decrease the amount of buyer's remorse by maintaining frequent contact with the new hire.

Send an announcement a few days before the new employee's arrival so they will be expected and can be greeted by their fellow employees. Make sure they have everything they will need to perform the job and have some meaningful task to perform on the first day.

Once you've made a good hire, the next component is to train the newcomer in the proper skills and the proper attitudes they need to have to be as effective as their potential allows.

PART D: TRAINING

Training: A Greater Bottom Line Issue than You Think

I once participated in a panel where one member shared with the group that *he doesn't train people* because he's afraid they might leave. Here's a scarier thought: What if they stay?

Research by the American Society for Training and Development has proven that training provides the highest return on investment in business today — higher than investments in equipment, buildings, or even technology.

> **High-performing credit unions prioritize investment in training.**

That's not to say that training for the sake of training is the answer. Poorly delivered and misdirected training will only frustrate your top performers.

How you deliver your training will make a huge and measurable impact on your growth. How do you get the best possible return from your invested dollars? Here are some suggestions on maximizing your return when you invest in training.

Know What You're Trying to Change

To start your training assessment, ask yourself, "What exactly is the problem? Are people lacking skills, or is it an attitude problem?"

A typical question asked by training professionals, barbaric as it sounds, is, "If a gun was held to their heads, would they be able to do this task?" If the answer is yes, it's not a skills-training issue. It's an attitude issue. You should alter your training approach based on which issue needs more attention.

Use the Right Method of Training

You want to use the least costly method of training that gets the best results. Often managers choose training methods because they are "hip" or new and later encounter results that are less than spectacular.

What are you trying to change? Skills can be learned through books, facilitator-led training sessions, and CD-ROM training. However, member service, sales culture, and similar issues are best learned by group training sessions.

Think of it this way: People are very driven by peer pressure. If an entire group is together discussing horrible telephone techniques while group members laugh and commiserate about how awful those behaviors are, it's difficult for an underperformer to go back and repeat the terrible phone techniques they've consistently used in the past. The gig is up!

To shift cultural behaviors, your two best options are trainer-led training or video-assisted training in which a leader's guide tells your untrained facilitator exactly what to do.

Bringing in a trainer is always a more expensive approach but can be very valuable if that person is skilled at shifting mindsets and building enthusiasm instead of just delivering information.

Depending upon the quality of the leader's guide that accompanies video training, this can be a good choice. The added benefit is that the trained person becomes an extreme advocate for change; you have an internal cheerleader long after an outside trainer leaves.

Don't waste your resources on video training that employees passively watch and that doesn't ask them to make commitments or create standards. It will only create a small and short-lived change.

It should be emphasized that training must address skill-set deficits, but it also must address any attitudinal issues people have that interfere with committing themselves to doing what you're asking.

It should also be stressed that peer pressure does wonders to influence behavioral change. Whenever possible, train in as large a group as is feasible. With the exception of skills training, most training gets better results when it's behavior focused. When you have employees who aren't doing what they should, don't single them out. Instead, point out their infractions in front of their peers. It's amazing how much the offenders suddenly want to be in compliance. They don't want to stand out and be recognized by their peers as someone who doesn't "get it."

Train Your Newbies Before They Sink the Ship

New employees who don't receive immediate training on cultural issues will do two things: First, they'll become much more difficult to train after several weeks and months. Second, they'll impact the more tenured employees who now feel there is no need for everyone to consistently do things *they* don't think are important, although you said they were. Video training on member service and sales culture issues should consistently be built into the first week's training for all new employees, as it is the least expensive way to deliver immediate training.

Measure and Celebrate

After the training, ask trainees to make commitments about what they'll do differently as a result of the training session. Have them sign a form in writing. Keep the form on file and go back to it often to see how they're doing on the commitment. Bring it out for performance reviews. Inspect what you expect!

Mystery Shop, measure, and celebrate employees' commitments to show them you fully intend to make sure they continue to be all they can.

Offer Certifications

People are driven to completion. Create a training system that allows them to earn a certificate. Gen-Xers, even more so than boomers, want and demand training that will add to their list of achievements. Provide that opportunity for them.

As an organization, you need to demand results from training. Let your people know you will provide training, you expect great things, and you will measure the results.

When creating your training budget, ask yourself the scary question: If you don't invest in training and they stay, what will THAT cost you?

Reward Effectively

For as long as I've gone to financial institution meetings, the same belief systems have been shared about "incentive programs." I'm not sure where the concept came from, but the ideas that have been touted in credit unions have been, at a minimum, ineffective and, in reality, often create dysfunction, greed, or disincentive.

Paying "per item sold," "per referral," or higher incentives during "campaigns" create havoc. Jealousy, infighting, and short-lived results are <u>not</u> what you want.

What we know in retrospect is that campaigns tend to bring up sales in that product area during the campaign, but they create no sustainable result. Individual incentives breed unhealthy relationships between employees, whereas team incentives get people rallied behind the overall results.

I've explored the incentive programs of many of the top-performing financial institutions and know one thing for sure: Nobody really has the answer. The only elements that seem to stand out are:

- Team incentives tend to be the most productive, and a combination of team and individual incentives seems to work well.
- Tracking information needs to be shared often, at least weekly. People need to know how they're doing compared to where they need to be.
- If tracking feels negative, blaming, or guilt ridden as opposed to inspiring and motivating, it will cause more

harm than good. The message needs to be delivered in an inspiring way.

- Top performers should receive bonuses that reward not only their individual contributions but also their contributions to the team. You want top performers leveraging their talent to bring others along.
- Be careful what your incentives are because they will have long-lasting implications. For example, mortgage lenders whose incentives are based on the volume of closed business but who are asked to do cross-sales will not pay much attention to your words. Also, if you focus on monetary incentives as opposed to adding other intrinsic incentives, you will create a culture of greed in which employees will leave you on a whim for a better monetary offer — and take their business with them.

Give careful thought to how you build your reward systems. Research shows that employees who are earning reasonable pay tend to be far more motivated by feeling that they are a part of something great and that their contribution matters. Managers often make the mistake of believing that compensation is at the very top when it comes to what motivates employees. Research shows employees, as long as they receive compensation that is reasonable, actually list compensation as not even being among the top seven motivators.

Freeing up the Future of Underperformers

I've never heard a manager complain about letting an underperformer go too quickly. In fact, it seems we usually know if someone is going to cut it by the end of the first day. We then start down the delusional path of trying to justify our decision by thinking that perhaps they're just slow to get started.

There are two roadblocks to letting underperformers go. First, we hate to believe we made the hiring mistake. Second, we are fearful of addressing the situation for a multitude of reasons, including that it is uncomfortable and we feel sorry for the person who doesn't fit. Many also are afraid of legal implications.

We discussed earlier that the legal implications are often more of an illusion in our mind. The real question is how to create a win-win departure.

Try thinking outside the traditional mindset that "firing" someone is a painful, ugly event that destroys the person involved. Often, pointing someone in a different direction can be one of the kindest acts.

Again, I'd ask you to challenge the conventional wisdom that says you have to hold a blame session that explains what's wrong. If you're managing properly, the employee already has been counseled on the areas where he or she is not doing well.

Try this win-win approach:

"It's critical that everyone who works here gets to bring all of their talents, their passion, and their skills to work every day and leave at the end of the day energized and excited with the results they create. It's obvious to me that we're not the place that allows you to thrive — and you deserve that.

"It's important that you find work that fills your life in positive ways. Life is too short to not be stimulated and receive joy from your work."

Depending on the maturity of the person and the work that they do, you may want to offer to let them stay for another few weeks while they look for a job that better fits them.

I have heard only positive outcomes from those whom I have coached on this topic. People don't sue because they're fired. They sue because they feel unjustly treated. The two are not the same. Most wrongful termination suits have no legitimate claims.

People seem very relieved to be treated with respect and in a way that allows them to save face.

Underperforming and toxic employees not only impact their own performance, but they lower the standards for everyone around them. There is often a sigh of relief when the person leaves, and the remaining employees are thrilled that the standards are now reinforced. Top performers are annoyed and unmotivated by those who slide by.

Go after the best possible people, train them to be extraordinary, and quickly admit the mistakes. Move toward bringing in team members that share the same core values and desires to make an impact.

Summary

You can create and build a staff of top performers. Smart credit unions know that their most important asset is their staff of well-hired, well-trained, passionate, and committed people. It's much easier to attract and keep high-quality employees when they feel part of something extraordinary.

Top-performing leaders who obtain great results from their people head up value-driven organizations. The core values of top performing organizations are the following:

Value Number 1: "No-Excuses Leadership"
Value Number 2: Hitting Conflict Head-On
Value Number 3: Playful Celebration
Value Number 4: Sense of Urgency
Value Number 5: Deeper-level Truth Telling
Value Number 6: High Expectations

Start with the Right People.
Financial institutions today are beset with high rates of turnover, under-performance, salespeople with no aptitude for sales, employee litigation, wrongful hiring claims, employee theft, and on and on. These risks are increased exponentially when you hire the wrong person and are greatly lessened when you hire, train, and retain the right people.

Part A: Recruit great employees by first defining the position and writing great ads.
1. Spell out EXPECTED ACCOMPLISHMENTS.
2. Spell out THE FUTURE.
3. Omit DETAILS of qualifications.
4. Lead with a GRIPPING TITLE.
5. Quickly DISQUALIFY.

Part B: Interview effectively by focusing on past performance.
An effective interview can uncover the common characteristics of most top performers. What you ultimately want to determine is if they have a track record of high energy and team leadership, a demonstrated record of comparable past performance, and a strong ability to adapt and produce in a new environment. Do this by asking powerful interview questions, implementing psychological testing, and doing a complete background check.

Part C: Hiring by asking the right questions and appraising the answers objectively.
Listen to what the candidate actually says. Resist the temptation to hear what you want to hear.

Part D: Train and manage the heart. Training is a bottom line issue.
You can't go wrong on an investment in effective training. Don't just train to be training. Know what you need to change. Define the problem and train to achieve desired results. Measure and celebrate the results of the training immediately. Offer certifications. Reward frequently.

Action Plan for Implementing Strategies in Chapter 7

Action to Take	Responsible Person	Results	Start Date	Target Date

Benefits

APPENDIX

Your Breakthrough Marketing Plan

No nonsense, Fast and Guaranteed Plan to Get and Keep More Members

Marketing is one of the most misunderstood functions of any business. The purpose of marketing is to educate potential members to succeed and make them confident that you can help. Every aspect of your business should be directly related to your marketing — or I should say that your marketing should be reflective of every aspect of your business.

Specifically, marketing includes your strategy and your strategic planning, your vision, your position, positioning and USP, your competition, your target market, your offer, your guarantee, and the marketing tools available to you. These are broadly perceived as the three general marketing activities: advertising, public relations, and promotions.

However, effective marketing really has much more to do with developing lasting member/staff relationships. A satisfied member is the best person you can spend your marketing dollars on and is your best marketer. Your staff should be trained to sell more and more often to your existing members and to reward those current members for bringing new members to you. That is the essence of true marketing.

You have probably heard the saying . . .
"Without marketing there are no sales.
Without sales there is no business."

You have probably also heard,

> **"There is no better way to find the real solution to a problem than to ask the right questions."**

I have found that the right questions should conform to a critical set of guidelines for success. Here they are:

Guidelines for Successful Marketing

1. Do EVERYTHING to get a member once…and then have an ***in-depth plan to bond to them for life*** by bringing all of their business to you.

2. Decisions to buy are ALWAYS made subconsciously.

3. Repetition impacts the unconscious.

4. It is critical to make EACH member feel unique.

5. Rank prospects A, B, and C. Spend marketing dollars only on the A's and those with the real potential of becoming A's.

6. Always focus the majority (at least 60 percent) of your marketing dollars on marketing to existing members.

7. Your highest return on investment allies are your employees, your members, and your partners who market with you.

EXTRAORDINARY CREDIT UNIONS

8. The *biggest mistake in marketing* is indifference after the sale.

9. Your ultimate objective is brand name awareness.

10. Without a marketing calendar, you have no marketing plan.

These ten principles of effective marketing should always be in the forefront as you develop your marketing plan. If questions are the foundation of determining your marketing success, and they are, then the structure is your marketing plan.

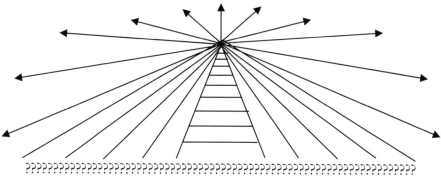

Your marketing plan should be question based and planned to get the results you wish to achieve: to reach your target market in all arenas.

Without an effective marketing plan your marketing will be hit or miss. The results of unplanned marketing are often disastrous and can be the reason for loss, not gain. Spontaneous, unplanned marketing is usually very costly and will yield disappointing results.

Develop Your Marketing Strategy

Don't follow the past, because most strategic plans are completely devoid of strategy. Your strategy should maximize service, retain members, penetrate each account for maximum growth, and position your credit union in your market area as clearly superior to others in the area. This will drive more growth.

> *"You can't win when playing a game defined by your competitors."*

How do you create the ultimate strategy?

Don't do what others in your industry are doing. Be unique.

This area is extremely important, so I am going to repeat what I said previously. You must plan your marketing strategy to get the results you need. List the highest performing companies, both within and outside your industry, that have created powerful and sustainable results. Look to companies like Southwest Airlines, Walgreens, Intel, Great Clips, Nordstrom, Domino's Pizza, and others that have excelled in certain areas.

For each company, list the strategies they employ. Ask, "How are they accomplishing it?"

You should list at least 50 strategies. Then you can evaluate those from which you want to borrow and combine two or more to create your ultimate strategy.

Don't forget to work backward by understanding what you really want to have happen. Ask yourself questions such as:

- ❑ Do you want to be progressive in the area of technology?
- ❑ Do you want to be high-touch and have a large staff to accommodate?
- ❑ Do you want to be a high-volume credit union with high efficiencies but less service?

Changing your strategy, if properly deployed, managed and systematized, can double, triple, or quadruple your rate of growth.

Your strategy can revitalize your people by enrolling them in a bigger picture of greatness. It breathes life into what is often a tired approach and exponentially increases the return from your resources. Now is the time to plunge in and develop your marketing strategies.

Marketing Strategy Worksheets

The following worksheets will help you develop a marketing plan that gets results. Prior to each worksheet I have given a review of information that I have covered more in-depth in the previous sections. Take time to fill in the blanks to this follow-the-formula marketing plan.

Your Strategies Worksheet

Strategy 1 (Example) Great Clips: standardized system for fast cut, guarantee results, have staff on call for busy times.

Strategy 2

Strategy 3

Strategy 4

Strategy 5

Strategy 6

Strategy 7

Strategy 8

Strategy 9
Strategy 10
Strategy 11
Strategy 12
Strategy 13
Strategy 14
Strategy 15
Strategy 16

Strategy 17

Strategy 18

Strategy 19

Strategy 20

Strategy 21

Strategy 22

Strategy 23

Strategy 24

Strategy 25

Strategy 26
Strategy 27
Strategy 28
Strategy 29
Strategy 30
Strategy 31
Strategy 32
Strategy 33
Strategy 34

Strategy 35

Strategy 36

Strategy 37

Strategy 38

Strategy 39

Strategy 40

Strategy 41

Strategy 42
Strategy 43
Strategy 44
Strategy 45
Strategy 46
Strategy 47
Strategy 48

Strategy 49

Strategy 50

What combination of strategies would give you the ultimate advantage and set you apart from your competitors?

_____
_____
_____
_____
_____
_____

Research Your Competition

Competitor 1:

Features:

Benefits:

Special offers:

Special products:

Weaknesses:

Competitor 2:

Features:

Benefits:

Special offers:

Special products:

Weaknesses:

Competitor 3:

Features:

Benefits:

Special offers:

Special products:

Weaknesses:

Your Credit Union:

Features:

Benefits:

Special offers:

Special products:

Weaknesses:

Benefits of Doing Business with You

When trying to find out what your target audience wants, it's important to know which of their basic needs to meet. Put a check mark by those that are most important to your market.

Some Basic Needs That Cause Members To Respond

- ❏ Security
- ❏ Saving time
- ❏ Conformity
- ❏ Power
- ❏ Profit
- ❏ Savings or economy
- ❏ Pride of ownership
- ❏ Comfort
- ❏ Convenience
- ❏ Social status
- ❏ Power

- ❏ Independence
- ❏ Health and well-being
- ❏ Friendship
- ❏ Love
- ❏ Other: _____
- ❏ Other: _____
- ❏ Other: _____
- ❏ Other: _____
- ❏ Other: _____
- ❏ Other: _____
- ❏ Other: _____

Your Benefits

Make a thorough list of all the benefits to your members from doing business with you.

The more benefits you have, the more potential members you will have who will be excited to do business with you. Although having a multitude of benefits is important, you need to focus on your **PRIMARY** one.

Three Examples:

> We have a team approach to calling on members so that our members have the safety of knowing that several people understand their needs and can help them.
>
> We have Saturday hours to provide convenience and save people valuable work time.
>
> We know our members' names so they feel welcome.

List Your Benefits:

_____
_____
_____
_____
_____
_____
_____
_____
_____
_____

Circle the benefits that are the most critical reasons why people would switch to you. Star the primary one upon which you will focus first.

Your Competitive Advantage

List below the most critical advantages that make you stand out from your competitors and those that **MATTER MOST** to your potential members and members.

Be very careful to be diligent in the quality of this answer, because this is the cornerstone you'll use as the basis for your entire marketing approach and campaign.

List Your Competitive Advantages

_____
_____
_____
_____
_____
_____
_____
_____
_____
_____
_____
_____
_____
_____
_____
_____

Articulate the value that is most important to you:
Examples: ***McDonald's: consistency; FedEx: commitment to on-time delivery***

_____
_____
_____
_____
_____
_____

Markets to Target

Most credit unions do "throw-it-against-the-wall-and-see-if-it-sticks" marketing where all their messages are global. Dollars that are spent on this type of global message and global audience are inefficiently spent resulting in extremely low returns. It's better to identify the different markets you will pursue and decide on the different tactics and messages you will use for each market. List as many markets as you can.

Examples can be realtors, technology companies, hospitals, mid-size businesses, company executives, hospital executives, hospital technicians, service-firm presidents, lawyers, etc. Be specific.

Also be specific for each department. For example, a commercial lender could target fast-growth businesses, service businesses, family-owned businesses, professional service firms, and many other businesses.

You could focus on those with special needs: two-salary families with children, senior citizens in deluxe senior housing, etc.

List Your Markets:

_____

Circle those niches that create the most opportunity for you in their likelihood to buy. You can choose several, but not so many that you lose focus.

Unique Selling Proposition

Your USP is the way you explain yourself AGAINST your competition.

Examples:

Domino's: Fresh, hot pizza delivered in 30 minutes or less, guaranteed.

Macaroni Grill: Great Italian value with "formal elegance and casual comfort" and a playful delivery.

Chrysler: Driver's-side airbag (worked great until competitors caught up).

Wedding Day Jeweler: The largest selection of wedding rings.

Red Rust Stopper: Stops rust each time you flush.

StepSafe Ice and Snow Remover: Melts ice and snow on walkways in super-low temperatures.

Your USP can be based on anything, including location, hours, price, product approach, celebrity endorsement, and delivery approach. It should not be ambiguous, such as "member service" or "home-town credit union."

Three Necessities of a Kick-butt USP

1. Member's perspective

Explain in a single sentence what's in it for the member. From the member's perspective . . .

- Is the message specific about what's in it for them?
- Is the benefit obvious and clear?
- Is the concept clearly unique compared to what your competitors are offering?
- If you were a new member, would the idea be exciting enough to entice you?

2. Dramatic difference

Is the difference dramatic?
- Is your difference evolutionary or revolutionary?
- Is your difference relevant?
- Does your difference generate real news?
- Does your difference create value perceived to be substantial compared to the cost?

Examples of dramatic differences for vodka (a clear, tasteless, odorless commodity by its very nature):

- Quadruple distilled from organically grown grain
- Made from American grain using four-column distillation
- Made from Polish rye
- Charcoal filtered in Belgium's oldest distillery
- Distilled in small batches

3. Reason to believe due to OVERT benefit

Benefit: Durable car polish   **Overt benefit:** Car polish keeps water beading for 90 days

Benefit: Fast car wash   **Overt benefit:** 60-second car wash

Benefit: Protects your car   **Overt benefit:** Under-carriage flush protects from salt damage

Benefit: Pest control   **Overt benefit:** Kills pests yet safe for pets

Your USP

_____
_____
_____
_____
_____

Power-charging Your USP with a Guarantee:

When you take the risk away from the member, they will believe your marketing and be far more likely to buy. You can tell people you're fast all day long, but when you say, "We guarantee you'll be waited on in our drive-thru within 5 minutes or we'll give you a $20 bill," people believe it.

Examples of successful guarantees from all industries:

Loan approval decision within 24 hours for all loans up to $250M or you pay no origination fee.

Complete satisfaction or the room is on us.

We'll use your name at least once or we'll give you a free movie pass.

We'll serve your food within 10 minutes or your dessert is on us.

Your Guarantee

Write your guarantee. Make sure that it stimulates a core value of why people buy from you and that it's legal.

_____

_____

_____

_____

101 Marketing Tools

Be methodical in selecting the best marketing tools for you. Circle all those you will use this year and then rank the top FIVE tools you will focus the most energy on to get the results you want.

1. Community involvement
2. Association memberships
3. Flexibility
4. Payment terms
5. Supporting a cause (homeless shelter, battered women's shelter, Boys and Girls Clubs, etc.)
6. Free consultations
7. Hours of operation
8. Days of operation
9. Inside signage
10. Outside signage
11. Business cards
12. Theme

13. Stationery
14. Identity
15. Logo/mime (visual depiction of concept)
16. Name of company
17. Niche market
18. Marketing plan
19. Marketing calendar
20. Toll-free number
21. Direct-dial phones
22. Phone etiquette and attitude
23. "Easy to do business with"
24. Reputation
25. Credibility
26. Brand name awareness
27. Speed
28. Posters
29. Testimonials
30. Research studies (you do on your own)
31. Direct mail postcards
32. Special events
33. Buying a mailing list of prospects
34. Radio spots
35. TV
36. Newspaper ads
37. Contests with prizes
38. Upgrade opportunities
39. Reprints
40. Networking
41. Satisfied members
42. Competitiveness
43. Member mailing list
44. Contagious enthusiasm
45. Sales training

46. Software to aid salespeople to track and focus on prospects
47. Location
48. Brochures
49. Telemarketing
50. Guarantee
51. Referral program
52. Online promotions
53. E-zine (e-mail magazine that adds value to the member)
54. Media contacts
55. Competitive advantages
56. Speaking at clubs
57. List benefits
58. How you greet (standard approach for saying hello and goodbye)
59. Newsletter
60. Published articles
61. Published column
62. Past success stories
63. Employee attire
64. Gifts
65. Catalog
66. Giving promotional items
67. Free seminars
68. Free parties and events
69. Sending mail that contains helpful information instead of sending marketing pieces
70. Trade shows
71. Amount of contact time with members
72. Gift certificates
73. Unique selling proposition
74. Joint marketing with alliances (dry cleaners, attorneys, CPAs)
75. E-mail

76. Humans answering phones
77. Public relations plan
78. Classified ads
79. Yellow pages
80. Member questionnaire to find out all of their needs
81. Follow-up person to thank members for opening accounts and cross-sell thoroughly
82. Scheduled calls for mortgage applicants to set up a meeting to switch all of their accounts prior to closing
83. Cross-sales system
84. Internal referral system
85. All staff trained to turn rate inquiries into conversations about needs and a system developed and managed
86. Schedule calls after opening accounts
87. Schedule mailings
88. Giving away information
89. Web site
90. Video or DVD
91. Giving free advice in hardcopy
92. Keyword Web strategy
93. Community celebrations
94. Free financial planning
95. Quarterly reviews
96. Articles or columns
97. Bounce-back cards
98. Press releases
99. Newsletters
100. Member center of influence breakfasts with speaker
101. Article reprints sent to members or potential members

One-Page Marketing Plan

The more succinct your marketing plan, the more effective it will be. Boil your marketing plan down to SEVEN sentences. Only the fourth sentence can be a long sentence.

Benefits we will stress are:

Target audiences we will pursue include:

Primary marketing tools we will use are:

Our USP will be:

Our brand will create an identity of:

Our Moments of Truth around our USP will include:

Our marketing budget as a percentage of our sales will be:

Other Necessary Marketing Plan Sections

Priority Plan of Marketing Tools

Prioritize the marketing tools you've chosen to use. Include the date you will begin and the person who is responsible for each.

Follow-up Plan

THIS IS CRITICAL. Unless you consistently follow up with members, your marketing efforts will not give you the growth you deserve. This plan needs to begin with an immediate thank you note, followed by a letter 30 days later asking about the member's satisfaction and offering to help with other needs. The plan should continue to describe how you will stay in touch for decades.

_____
_____
_____
_____
_____
_____
_____

Marketing Calendar

If a day without orange juice is like a day without sunshine, a marketing plan without a marketing calendar is just a hope and a dream.

To put substance to your marketing plan, make sure each week has a column for the market you're going after, which product is being promoted, and which marketing tools you'll be using. It's optimal to plan for the entire year, although only the first three months should be cast in stone because market changes may necessitate alterations.

_____
_____
_____
_____
_____
_____
_____
_____
_____

Member Referral Plan

Put a person in charge of implementing a plan to help you focus on getting new members from old members. The plan should involve asking for referrals immediately at the time of the sale, six and twelve months later, and every year thereafter.

_____
_____
_____
_____

Centers-of-Influence Referral Plan

One source, such as an attorney, a realtor, a CPA, or a board member, could send you 20 to 30 percent of your business. Create your plan to identify your strongest potential centers of influence, stay in touch with them, and make them look good for referring you.

_____
_____
_____
_____
_____

Credibility Plan

Seminars, articles, columns, and speeches for local groups are just a few of the ways you can position yourself as "the source" — and the best one at that. When speaking or writing, do NOT sell — tell them only how they can improve their lives by knowing your information. Reprints of your articles could be copied and sent to your prospects as a way to get their attention and to your members as a way to keep in touch and bring more value.

_____
_____
_____
_____
_____

Media Plan

Use only the media that, based on your own survey, you know your member pays attention to. Although money invested in most of the other tools we've talked about here will usually give you a far better return, some media advertising can solidify the work you're doing elsewhere.

_____
_____
_____
_____
_____

Competitor Research Plan

List how often you will research your competition, what you will shop, who will do it, how the information will be delivered, and how you will build in the flexibility to adjust to the changing market.

_____
_____
_____
_____
_____

Potential Member/Member Research Plan

Create your own questionnaire asking your members what they most want from you, what they want for themselves, where they would expect to hear from you, what's important to them in a business relationship with you, why they came to you, and what they would want you to add or eliminate. Create a plan to survey a random sample of those who come into your credit union, send direct mail to some, and ask similar questions to potential members.

_____
_____
_____
_____
_____
_____

Technology Plan

How will you use technology to streamline your marketing processes? List what software you will use to keep track of potential members, what fields you will capture, how you will use e-mail to stay in contact, etc. Also include how you will use your member database to better cross-sell them to create a deeper relationship.

_____
_____
_____
_____
_____
_____

Complaint-Resolution Process

Every complaint is a gift because we know, through national research, that only 4 percent of those who have complaints speak up. The rest tell others and create negative public relations, and/or they leave. Knowing this, it's critical to create a plan to learn from each complaint, reward the person who complains, and create an even closer relationship with that member.

Immediately letter of apology to mbr - postmarked the day he came in

After cool-off period, about a week, send special offer to compensate for trouble

Converting Shoppers Plan

On average, a person who shops you is far more interested than those who don't. Quoting them your pricing and sending them on their merry way is almost criminal. Have a plan to handle each person who shops you. Ask the questions that get the conversation off pricing and onto your benefits, to capture their information, to follow-up, and eventually to capture all of their business.

Sales System

Without a sales system that identifies the exact sales questions each department is to ask, how the information should be recorded, how you will cross-sell, how you will track cross-sales, what you measure, etc., any "sales training" you do will produce only short-term results.

The days of "features and benefits" training are dead.

List the sales forms that need to be completed; the person or department that compiles and disseminates opportunities for other areas; how you will identify a member or potential member as an A, B, or C; and how you will communicate differently to each of those categories.

Your Brand

You MUST stand out and be known for the values you uphold:

Outrageous, sexy, chameleon — Madonna
Compassionate, spiritual, enlightened — Oprah

Quality — Toyota and Honda
Driving — BMW
Engineering — Mercedes
Speed — Ferrari

Words, Words, and More Words

What you say and how you say it are vitally important to the effectiveness of your marketing. Studies have shown that certain words outsell other words 100 to one. The following are great advertising words that attract potential members and draw them to you. Use them well and frequently in all of your marketing materials.

Important Magic Words

Free	Proud
New	Healthy
You	Safe
Sale	Right
Introducing	Security
Save	Winnings
Money	Fun
Discover	Value
Results	Advice
Easy	Wanted
Proven	Yours truly,
Guaranteed	People
Love	Why
Benefits	Improvement
Alternative	Sensational
Now	Revolutionary
Win	Miracle
Gain	Magic
Test worthy	Quick
Good looking	Wanted
Comfortable	Bargain
Breakthrough	Hurry

Your Headlines

No one will go beyond the headline to see what you offer or guarantee if the headline does not hook the reader instantly. The headline is the most important message you can create in your sales letter or ad. Take time to craft a great headline and then test it to see that it works. Keep refining it. But when you find one that works, use it in all your advertising copy. Remember that repetition is the key to effective advertising. All advertising is a game of playing copycat with a twist. Though you want your USP to be unique, you can apply successful headlines to your product or service and find ongoing success. Here are some great headlines that have proven their worth over and over.

All Time Best Headline Templates:

- A little mistake that could [ruin years of savings]
- A little mistake that can [cost you a fortune]
- Seven secrets for [increasing your income]
- Seven ways to [get richer] almost instantly
- Five no-fail strategies for _____
- Nine sure ways to _____
- Nine questions you must ask _____ and the one that will separate _____ from _____
- A startling fact about _____
- A new way to _____ that has never failed
- An announcement of unusual importance to every _____
- Five simple ways to _____
- How to avoid the 10 biggest [financial mistakes]
- How to bounce back from _____
- How to make the most of your [current financial situation]
- How to react to _____

- How to think like a _____: The 3 things you MUST do
- How to sell against your competition…and always win
- How to win over a _____
- How to transform your ideas into reality
- A new way to _____ that has never failed
- The amazing _____ that will change our life forever
- The 17 ways to _____
- Five great _____ and what they can teach you about how to _____
- Secrets of ancient _____
- No more _____
- The amazing secret that _____
- The best-kept _____ secrets in _____
- The case for _____
- The can't-miss system for _____
- The four legendary _____ and what they had in common
- The E.N.T. principle
- The last word on _____
- The number one (#1) most powerful _____
- The one most important piece of _____ advice you'll ever get
- The proven formula for _____
- The _____ phenomenon and what it means to you
- The Ten Commandments of _____
- The simple formula for _____
- The three people you have to speak to about _____
- The ugly truth about _____
- The very best _____ money can buy

Your Marketing Pieces

Entire books are written on each area of marketing, advertising, promotion, and public relations. There are so many variables and so many activities we could discuss that I could give you an additional 1,000 pages of detailed how-to's, and we would still not cover everything. But I am sure that is not what you want. Therefore, I have selectively presented on our Web site, www.EmmerichFinancial.com, the samples of key marketing pieces that, when adapted to your credit union, will serve you well in constructing your own pieces or in helping you evaluate the work of your PR/advertising firm. These include a highly successful sales letter that can serve as the foundation for all your print materials, a killer ad, and other marketing pieces.

Just remember that the key in all advertising is to TEST results before you roll out a major marketing campaign.

Summary

Your marketing is essential to your success. All of your marketing has to be in line with all aspects of your entire business. This includes your strategy, your vision, your position, your USP, and your guarantee. There are many marketing tools that can serve your best interests and attract potential members to explore your offering. Of course, the best marketing is directed toward your existing members to get them to use your services more often and to use more of them. They should also be rewarded when they bring new members to your credit union.

Whether you are writing a special report as a giveaway, a postcard, sales letter, advertisement, banner, or Web site, you need to place the primary benefit first and then support it with benefits related to it. If you make all your marketing benefits loaded, then it will appeal to your target market and draw them to your credit union.

Plan your marketing calendar with specific activities at specific times for specific success.

Marketing Action Plan

Action to Take	Responsible Person	Results	Start Date	Target Date

Benefits

Index

'How' questions, 178
'Order-taking', 198
Abe Lincoln, 128
Advertising, 17, 79, 85, 91, 98, 113, 114, 135, 136, 144, 145, 150, 159, 173, 198, 228, 251, 281, 285, 286, 288
AIDA formula, 143
Allen, 124
Allen, Robert G., 124
American Management Association, 231
American Research Group, 83
American Society for Training and Development, 237
Authentic marketing, 133
Background check, 246
Bank of America, 82, 83, 89, 91
Beckwith, 78
Bill Gates, 64
BMW, 81, 284
Body copy, 145, 147
Budget, 12, 57, 115, 156, 157, 218, 220, 240, 294
Cadillac, 81
Caples, 146
Carlson, 24, 25
Celebration, 36, 194, 214, 215, 245
Closing question, 184
Collins, 13, 206
Commerce Bank, 13, 99
Commitment, 15, 26, 34, 49, 75, 133, 134, 174, 203, 205, 210, 240, 268
Communication, 39, 75, 80, 90, 127, 150, 212
Conceptual thinkers, 168
Conflict, 203, 206, 210, 211, 213, 245
Correspondence, 27, 28, 40, 42, 132, 195
Covey, 68
Creating a buzz, 121, 124

Creating a strategy, 85, 101
Creating a system, 169, 191
Cross-sales, 186, 187, 189, 190, 191, 242, 276, 284
Cross-sales system, 187, 276
Customer retention, 11, 17, 137, 158
David Ogilvy, 145
Deming method, 74
depression, 68, 69, 208
Depression, 68, 69, 208
Direct mail, 135, 136, 137, 138, 140, 142, 143, 144, 152, 154, 155, 274, 282
Dr. Robert Cialdini, 153
Dr. Seuss, 204
Excuses, 9, 11, 34, 75, 202, 203, 204, 205
FedEx, 86, 87, 93, 268
Gates, 64
Gladwell, 121
Good to Great, 13, 206
Harry Beckwith, 78
Headline, 141, 145, 146, 148, 152, 286
High expectations, 35, 220, 245
Hiring, 38, 136, 217, 222, 223, 231, 232, 234, 243, 245, 246
Incentive programs, 241
Interviewing, 133, 202, 223, 230
Jack Whittle, 185
James Patterson, 202
Jay Conrad Levinson, 125
Jim Collins, 13, 206
John Caples, 146
John F. Kennedy, 63
John Nash, 134
Johnson, 134
Kennedy, 63
Leaders, 13, 23, 57, 75, 85, 133, 168, 192, 201, 202, 203, 204, 208, 214, 245, 294
Leadership, 4, 8, 14, 24, 57, 80, 101, 107, 201, 202, 203, 205, 206,

207, 209, 218, 226, 228, 230, 245, 246, 294
Levinson, 125
Lincoln, 128
Macaroni Grill, 32, 270
Malcolm Gladwell, 121
Market research, 118
Marketing, 5, 11, 12, 17, 42, 59, 73, 75, 80, 81, 82, 83, 84, 85, 90, 91, 93, 98, 111, 112, 113, 114, 115, 116, 117, 119, 120, 121, 123, 124, 125, 126, 127, 128, 129, 133, 138, 139, 140, 141, 142, 143, 145, 149, 156, 157, 158, 159, 160, 173, 224, 226, 228, 251, 252, 253, 254, 255, 267, 268, 272, 273, 274, 275, 277, 278, 279, 282, 285, 288, 289, 294
Marketing tools, 251, 273, 278, 279, 289
Marlboro, 125, 126
Massey, 89
Mastermind, 124, 125
Member service, 8, 17, 23, 24, 27, 31, 33, 34, 38, 39, 49, 54, 65, 72, 113, 238, 240, 270
Mercedes, 81, 82, 173, 284
Mission statement, 54, 60, 61, 62, 64, 66, 67
Mistakes managers make, 192
Mitch Massey, 89
Models, 71
Moment of Truth, 24, 29, 31, 43, 44, 45, 46, 47, 48
Moments of Truth, 25, 27, 28, 35, 40, 49, 50
Most compelling words, 146
Mystery Shopping, 35, 36, 37, 38, 39, 217
Mystery Shopping Awards Program, 35
Nash, 134
Niche marketing, 125, 127, 128
Ogilvy, 145
Operational thinkers, 168
order-taking, 198

Passion, 13, 34, 69, 150, 208, 243, 294
Peer pressure, 26, 238, 239
Phone standards, 41
Position (statement of position), 78, 79, 81, 82, 85, 88, 93, 99, 124, 127, 129, 131, 183, 192, 204, 223, 231, 235, 236, 245, 251, 254, 280, 289
Positioning questions, 177, 181
Positioning statement, 78, 79, 80, 90, 92, 93
Psychological testing, 231, 232, 233, 246
Rate inquiries, 165, 169, 172, 173, 190, 191, 195, 276
Rate inquiry process, 173
Reasons to market, 158
Recruiting, 223, 225
Referral sources, 130, 132
Regina Roat, 232
Relationship marketing, 114
Roat, 232
Robert G. Allen, 124
Robert Johnson, 134
Saab, 32, 33, 81
Sales culture, 166, 167, 197, 203, 215, 238, 240
Sales letter, 136, 142, 145, 147, 151, 155, 286, 288, 289
Sales management, 106, 166, 226
Scandinavian Air, 24
Sense of urgency, 9, 144, 215, 216, 217, 245
Seuss, 204
Situational questions, 175, 176
SMART, 223
Southwest Airlines, 10, 97, 215, 254
Stephen Covey, 68
Sterling McCall Toyota, 232
Strategic planning, 8, 11, 102, 251
Strategic planning question, 102
Strategic Planning Questions, 102
Strategic thinkers, 168
Strategies, 5, 15, 17, 39, 51, 57, 59, 76, 82, 95, 99, 109, 111, 112, 114, 115, 116, 119, 156, 161,

199, 247, 254, 255, 256, 262, 286, 294
Strategy, 8, 11, 12, 18, 24, 27, 31, 49, 56, 58, 59, 60, 85, 97, 98, 99, 100, 101, 107, 108, 112, 115, 119, 121, 122, 125, 128, 132, 135, 137, 156, 251, 253, 254, 255, 256, 257, 258, 259, 260, 261, 262, 276, 289
Survey, 56, 138, 139, 140, 144, 235, 281, 282
Targeted mailing list, 137, 140
The Wall Street Journal Online, 235
Thinking styles, 168
Thompson, 65
Tommy Thompson, 65
Top-performing banks, 17, 120, 133, 137, 138, 194, 214, 241

Training, 14, 26, 28, 171, 184, 195, 207, 215, 223, 237, 238, 239, 240, 246, 274, 284
Unique Selling Proposition, 78, 80, 82, 90, 94, 275
USP, 78, 80, 84, 86, 87, 90, 91, 251, 270, 271, 272, 286, 289
Values, 11, 13, 63, 73, 74, 80, 102, 197, 201, 202, 222, 244, 245, 284
Vision, 5, 8, 20, 54, 58, 60, 62, 63, 64, 65, 66, 67, 68, 69, 70, 71, 73, 74, 75, 101, 102, 104, 251, 289
Volkswagen Beetle, 81
Volvo, 81
Whittle, 185
Worksheet, 87, 94, 255, 256

Other Financial Services Books and Learning Tools
by Roxanne Emmerich

FREE Newsletter: Sign up your entire leadership team for our *FREE GrowYourBank e-mail newsletter* filled with immediately useable sales and marketing strategies. Many leadership teams distribute it at their weekly leadership meeting for a discussion about implementation. Go to www.EmmerichFinancial.com.

Breakthrough Sales Meetings: Power charge your sales meetings with these learning tools designed to dramatically enhance the sales and service sets and mindsets of your team.

No-Mistakes Hiring Tools: Find out how one easy to use and inexpensive tool can help decrease your turnover by 67 percent while dramatically increasing the effectiveness of your team members by matching each person to the job where they can thrive.

Thank God It's Monday: How to Build a Motivating Workplace: A business best seller and book of outstanding merit that helps everyone in the workplace take accountability for the attitudes and results of the entire organization. Rekindle the passion for extraordinary results.

Sales Management and Marketing Bootcamp™: Almost every financial institution is dead wrong in their sales management and marketing approach. Find out shoestring budget approaches that surpass the expensive "traditional" marketing. Discover how to get more members, keep them for life, and do more business with everyone.

Permission to Be Extraordinary™ Summit: For top-performing leaders who are ready to be pushed to the next level.

Call 800-236-5885 for more information
on the tools that best fit your specific needs
or call to discuss how Roxanne can help you
develop success strategies and maximize results.

Submit Your Success Stories

I want to hear your stories of adventure, triumph, and success. When my son was learning to dive off the diving board, he yelled, "look at me" over 100 times in one day. As adults, we've learned to suppress that request for someone to praise our successes . . . but the need for someone to applaud remains.

When that feeling of bubbling over hits, please share your excitement here. My staff and I are energized and excited by the breakthroughs of our clients. It's how we learn, grow, and know that we're on the right path.

Contact me via e-mail:

**Roxanne@EmmerichGroup.com or
Call 800-236-5885**